MACONOCHIE'S GENTLEMEN

MACONOCHIE'S GENTLEMEN

The Story of Norfolk Island

&

The Roots of Modern Prison Reform

Norval Morris

OXFORD
UNIVERSITY PRESS
2002

OXFORD
UNIVERSITY PRESS

Oxford   New York

Athens   Auckland   Bangkok   Bogotá   Buenos Aires
Cape Town   Chennai   Dar es Salaam   Delhi   Florence   Hong Kong   Istanbul
Karachi   Kolkata   Kuala Lumpur   Madrid   Melbourne   Mexico City   Mumbai
Nairobi   Paris   São Paulo   Shanghai   Singapore   Taipei   Tokyo   Toronto   Warsaw

and associated companies in
Berlin   Ibadan

Copyright © 2002 by Oxford University Press, Inc.

Published by Oxford University Press, Inc.
198 Madison Avenue, New York, New York 10016

Oxford is a registered trademark of Oxford University Press

Library of Congress Cataloging-in-Publication Data
Morris, Norval.
Maconochie's gentlemen : the story of Norfolk Island
& the roots of modern prison reform / Norval Morris.
p.   cm. — (Studies in crime and public policy)
ISBN 0-19-514607-7
1. Maconochie, Alexander, 1787–1860.
2. Penal colonies—Norfolk Island—History.
3. Penal colonies—Great Britain—History.
4. Norfolk Island—History.
5. Prison reformers—Norfolk Island—Biography.
I. Title.   II. Series.
HV8950.N84 M335 2001   365'.99482—dc21   2001021377

Designed by Helen B. Mules

1 3 5 7 9 8 6 4 2

Printed in the United States of America
on acid-free paper

CONTENTS

CONTENTS

ACKNOWLEDGMENTS

I have been extraordinarily fortunate in those who helped me write this book.

The late Sir John Vincent Barry, of the Supreme Court of Victoria, Australia, was my teacher and friend; he remains a continuing and guiding stimulus, and his biography of Maconochie provided the basis of fact for this story.

James Jacobs of New York University, Michael Tonry of Cambridge University, and Franklin Zimring of the University of California at Berkeley, all three being leading scholars of crime and public policy, and all three my current mentors (time and their abilities have reversed our roles), advised and encouraged me to press on with this piece of fact/fiction during a long period of illness. My debt to them is beyond repayment.

Les Brown, a fine historian living on Norfolk Island, guided me to the convict past, and the tourist present, of that lovely island.

Dedi Felman of Oxford University Press, and Douglas Dennis,

now serving a life sentence in the Louisiana State Prison at Angola, were wise and efficient editors.

And my wife, Elaine, and our family, all nine of them, loved me and supported me during times when inattentive and moody abstraction characterized my demeanor.

Author's Note

Sometimes truth is seen from the corner of the eye; sometimes it is captured by considering current problems in a different historical and cultural setting. Thus the structure of this book: a fictional tale based on actual people and events that occurred in earlier times in a very remote place, followed by discussions of lessons that story holds for current imprisonment practices.

George Orwell's essay "A Hanging" gave me the model I have since followed. In it he describes the execution of a small Hindu man. On his way to the gallows, flanked by two solicitous warders, the prisoner steps slightly aside to avoid a puddle on the ground close to the execution block. Orwell then speculates in his usual incisive and elegant style on why that action brought home to him "the unspeakable wrongness of cutting a life short when it is in full tide."

Is Orwell's story true? Was there the hanging that he described? Was there a puddle and did the Hindu step around it? If so, why? Contemporary records may answer some of these questions, but only some. Of more relevance, do these questions matter?

The answer, of course, is that timeless psychological truth lies in Orwell's story. Perhaps District Officer Eric Blair, later to become renowned as George Orwell, witnessed these events when he served in Burma; perhaps not. But they certainly now live as psychologically true, just as Hamlet, the Prince of Denmark, will forever live at Elsinore.

"A Hanging" launched me on writing fiction that probed moral and social issues that interest me. It came to me that Orwell provided very little about the executed man, beyond describing him physically. Nothing about what he had done or been convicted of doing; nothing about why he had done it, if he had—nothing of his prior circumstances or his motives. He remained a shadow. The facts of his life were not necessary to Orwell's story. But that gap prompted me to try to fill in the man's story as a parable and it became the first chapter ("The Brothel Boy") of my book, *Madness and the Criminal Law*. Thus Eric Blair's vision became the foundation of my search by fiction for "truth."

Maconochie's Gentlemen portrays Captain Alexander Maconochie and his years on Norfolk Island in the same way. In my own life, I am much involved in prison issues. In this book I try to wrestle with some of these issues as they arose in Maconochie's island prison. Until his arrival, Norfolk Island had ranked in brutality and suffering with the French settlement on Devil's Island and the Russian settlement on the Sakhalin Islands (see Anton Chekhov's "A Journey to Sakhalin"). It was the most severe prison in the considerably severe range of then existing British prisons and gaols. The lash, the spreadeagle, the wooden gag, and the scavenger's daughter often accompanied prisoners to the dankest of cells.

This is not an unremittingly grim prison story. His wife and six children accompanied Maconochie to Norfolk Island. Much of the story is about these "other prisoners."

Is this a true story? The events in it are true. Contemporary records and letters, official and private, testify to their occurrence. I adhered closely to the historical records, relying on John Vincent Barry's *Captain Maconochie of Norfolk Island* (Oxford University Press, 1958) as my primary biographical guide. The story is true if I can achieve psychological truth in deploying the personal, social, and moral lives of the characters. It is based on facts, and shaped by intuition and speculation. After the story is told, I reveal who among my characters were in fact on the Island and who were not—or were they? I am unsure.

ABOUT THE AUTHOR

Professor Morris is one of the leading criminologists in the United States. Born in Auckland, New Zealand, and educated in Australia and England, he settled in the U.S. in 1964. He was the first researcher given access to English convict prisons in 1948 and has been steadily involved with prisons, prison officials, and inmates ever since. He has been a member of the Task Force on Prisoner Rehabilitation under President Nixon; has served on several advisory commissions to the governor of Illinois; and had been special assistant to the attorney general of the United States under President Carter. He designed the overall program for the federal prison at Butner, North Carolina, and has worked closely with unjustly convicted inmates.

A former dean of the University of Chicago Law School, Morris is currently the Julius Kreeger Professor of Law and Criminology, Emeritus, at the University of Chicago. He has been the recipient of many research awards and has authored and coauthored several critically acclaimed books, including the recent *The Oxford History of the Prison*. Morris is coeditor with Michael Tonry of the Studies in Crime and Public Policy series published by Oxford University Press.

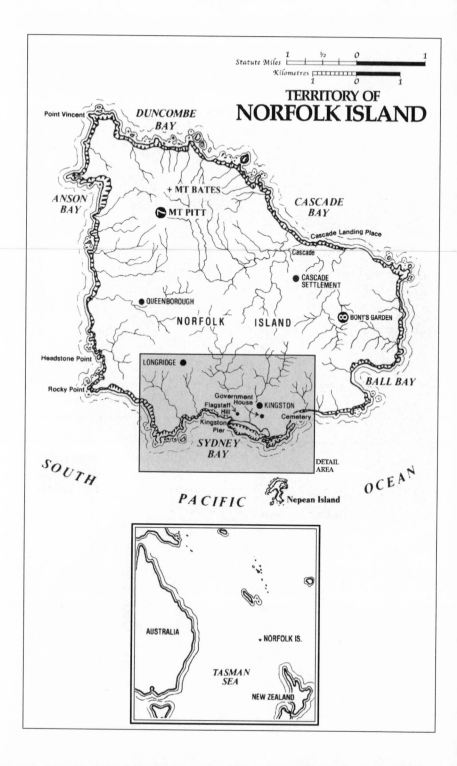

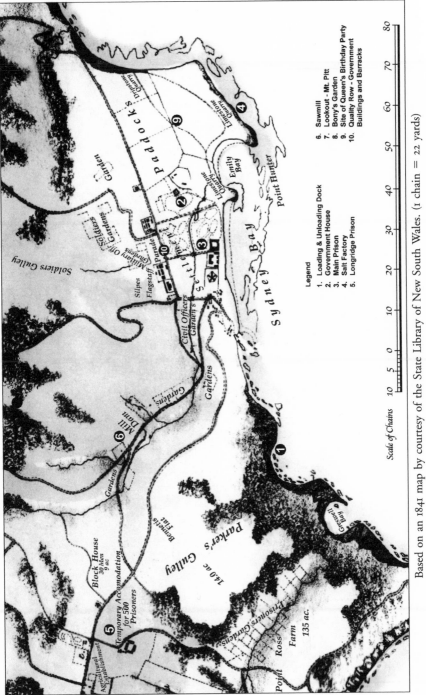

Based on an 1841 map by courtesy of the State Library of New South Wales. (1 chain = 22 yards)

Legend

1. Loading & Unloading Dock
2. Government House
3. Main Prison
4. Salt Factory
5. Longridge Prison
6. Sawmill
7. Lookout - Mt. Pitt
8. Bony's Garden
9. Site of Queen's Birthday Party
10. Quality Row - Government Buildings and Barracks

Scale of Chains   10 5   0   10   20   30   40   50   60   70   80

CAPTAIN ALEXANDER MACONOCHIE, R.N., K.H.
By E. V. Rippingille, 1836

MACONOCHIE'S GENTLEMEN

Being the story of
England's most punitive prison,
situated 1,000 miles off the east coast of Australia,
where were sent those who had been transported to Australia
as punishment for felony
and who committed further felonies in Australia
and were further transported to Norfolk Island,
to be most severely punished,
and of Captain Alexander Maconochie and his family
who for four years turned this living hell
into an orderly penal settlement,
and of the means of this achievement,
and of its relevance to today's excessive,
criminogenic, and costly
use of incarceration.

I am no sentimentalist. I most fully subscribe to the right claimed by society to make examples of those who break its laws, that others may feel constrained to respect and obey them. But individuals thus sacrificed to what is, at best, but a high political expediency (for vengeance belongs to another) have their claims on us also, claims only the more sacred because they are helpless in our hands. . . . We have no right to cast them away altogether. Even their physical suffering should be in moderation, and the moral pain we must and ought to inflict with it should be carefully framed so as if possible to reform, and not necessarily to pervert, them.

Punishment may avenge, and restraint may, to a certain limited extent, prevent crime; but neither separately, nor together, will they teach virtue. That is the province of moral training alone (including under this term everything which appeals to the mind, not to the body, as moral, religious, and intellectual instruction, progressive degrees of freedom according to conduct, and the abuse of these checked by motives drawn from self-interest, and other principles producing mental impulse, not by force, or the infliction of immediate punishment).

Captain Alexander Maconochie, R.N., 1838

Captain Maconochie avows his opinion that the first object of all Convict Discipline should be the Reformation of the Criminal. This opinion, however agreeable it may be to the dictates of humanity, is not, I believe, the received one of Legislators, who rather require as the first object of Convict Discipline that it should be a terror to Evildoers.

Sir George Gipps, 1840

[T]he mode of governing convicts lately suggested by Captain Maconochie might in part at least be attempted with advantage . . . it would be advisable to ascertain, by experiment, the effect of establishing a system of reward and punishment not founded merely upon the prospect of immediate pain or immediate gratification, but relying mainly upon the effect to be produced by the hope of obtaining or the fear of losing future and distant advantages.

Molesworth Committee, House of Commons, 1838

Part 1

NORFOLK ISLAND,
1840–1844

M emories, certainly my memories, do not flow evenly; they bounce about in time from scene to scene, and there are great gaps of remembrance. I try to establish sequence, to search for cause and consequence. Sometimes I seem to have made wise decisions, struck sensible postures, but often a wry sadness is all I find. Other times there are patches of clarity. It was clear that my daughter, Mary Ann, believed she was treated unfairly, misused, she said. I had no inkling of this until that Sunday morning at breakfast when she fixed her hostility to my plans sharply in my memory.

We were in the smaller room of the two used for dining in Government House. When the Franklins were there we needed the larger room with its grand mahogany table to seat the two Franklins and the eight Maconochies. But this morning Sir John and Lady Franklin were on a Governor's tour in the Northeast of Van Diemen's Land and my four sons were not yet up and about, being allowed to sleep in today before church.

There were only four of us at table: my wife, Mary, our daughters Mary Ann and Catherine, and myself. Mary Ann had awakened early as she often does, sometimes before dawn, and, since Government House overlooks the harbour, had seen a ship preparing to enter the harbour. She had walked down to help welcome the jolly boat and the mail from the ship and had brought the Government House mailbag back with her to our breakfast. I searched quickly through it to see if there was a communication to me from the Colonial Office. There was. It was what I very much wanted: The offer of the superintendence of Norfolk Island at a salary equal to that of a lieutenant-governor of a small colony.

It was not a movement order, posting me to Norfolk Island. It was phrased as an offer, should I desire it, and suggested that I might care to try out the scheme for the governance of convicts I had been writing about. If so (and I had the sense that the draftsmen of the document were of the view that I would be unwise to accept their offer—the tone was: you have written about your theories, see if you can make them work, we doubt it), instructions had been issued to Sir John Franklin, the Governor of Van Dieman's Land, and to Sir George Gipps, the Governor of New South Wales, to facilitate and expedite my assumption of this duty.

Excitedly, I shared the news with Mary and the girls. Mary and Catherine made no immediate reply. Not so Mary Ann.

"Are you really going to drag us all along to that terrible place, Father?" She seemed on the point of tears; I had not seen tears from her for several years. It was as if she had suddenly, not gently and sweetly, but suddenly and brusquely, taken on woman's estate. No longer a bright but uncertain child, she had in that moment become a mature and sharp-tongued woman.

I had known her for sixteen years by the pet name "Minnie" rather than the more formal "Mary Ann." I found in reply I used neither. I was now not confronted by my dear girl Minnie, but by an attractive and independent-minded young woman, Mary Ann: "You question our going to Norfolk Island after the three long months of our planning, without a word of objection from you?"

Now, clearly through tears, she managed to say; "No. Father, I esteem your purpose; it is your making us go with you that I resent."

The substance as well as the manner of her complaint surprised me. She had been the only member of the family who seemed at all interested in my evolving Marks System; indeed, she had helped me shape it by her probing questioning. I could not doubt her interest, but suddenly, as my theory became a reality for me, she wished to be free of it.

Recovering quickly, eyes now dry and hard, she developed her opposition to my plans for us on Norfolk Island. She had never before been so direct with me. She and I had discussed my Marks System and she had read and indeed helped me phrase my submissions and correspondence to England on the governance of convicts. I knew she was a skeptic; I knew she thought I overstated my case; I knew she believed that there were many prisoners who were unlikely to respond to my proposed system of gradual movement toward conformity, tested and marked by increments of freedom and duty; but she had never previously suggested, as this morning's outburst implied, that I was sacrificing our family to my theory of punishment.

I avoided any direct controversy at the table. I said that it was only an offer and that I would have to think about it, and talk with Mary, and then with my daughters and sons, but I knew I was dissimulating and I think Mary Ann also knew it.

I was glad that the Franklins were now absent, though he had been my closest friend before we accompanied him and Lady Franklin to Van Diemen's Land. We had both served as naval captains and been promoted on retirement to the rank of Commander. He had then continued his series of explorations of the Arctic, which brought him fame, while I had been one of his loyal supporters. I had thrown in my lot with him in the subservient role of his personal secretary (subservient because I had been senior to him in the Navy) when his appointment as Governor of Van Diemen's Land was announced, under the promise that a suitable post would be found for me in the southern colonies as soon as one became available. But the weeks grew to months and then to more than a year with nothing suitable available, and Sir John growing daily more distant from me due to his reaction to the servile fawning lavished upon him by the members of the Legislative Council and the dominant political faction in the colony who had, wisely, taken an instant dislike to me as an impediment to their control of the Governor.

As a naval officer and as a leader of Arctic expeditions, John had manifested remarkable judgment and coolness in many crises; as the lieutenant-governor of Van Diemen's Land he had manifested remarkably different qualities: a susceptibility to flattery and a willingness to believe in unreal, complex, political schemes directed against him, of which I was the supposed leader. Nevertheless, having to live so close together in the same household, as we did for the time being, we managed courteous relationships on the surface, greatly modulated by the encouraging warmth of Lady Franklin's affection for my family.

A colonial posting for me, which was not an embarrassing come-down, had until now seemed as distant as the day we

reached Hobart Town, whereas Norfolk Island offered an opportunity to prove in action the value of a theory of human
behavior which might well have lasting significance. And I
could not face the idea of crawling back to England as a failure—which is how our return would be seen. And, beyond
that, I hated the way convicts were being treated in New South
Wales and here in Van Diemen's Land, and it would be a joy
to demonstrate that life for them need not, indeed should not,
be so brutal.

Mary, I knew, would want to come with me and so would
the boys. No harm would come to the girls; they might miss
a year or two of the London social whirl, but they could return
to England in two or three years' time and be the better for
the antipodean experience. And Minnie in particular seemed
to be growing in mind and judgment at an unusually swift
pace, mainly, I flattered myself, stimulated by the unusual tuition I was giving her. Not the usual graces of the young lady,
for which Mary provided training—sewing, music and song,
dance, sketching—but serious studies in geography, Latin, and
philosophy under my tutelage. These should not be abandoned. No, we must go together as a family to Norfolk Island.

But at another level I knew I was deceiving myself—denying
what seemed obvious on much later reflection. Since her pu-
berty and the flowering of her unusual intelligence, Minnie
had been especially dear to me. She was the only one of the
family with whom I could really talk, other than about family
matters or personalities. Our conversations mostly involved my
plans, my punishment theories, my political difficulties and
what to do about them, matters which I could discuss with
no one else in this colony now that the rift had opened between Franklin and me.

I was sedulous in attending to her studies, but every such

session returned at the end to my Marks System and how it might be launched. I needed her on Norfolk Island.

But that too seemed self-deception. On the Island there would surely be senior military officers who would welcome such discussions under the pressure of the reality test of my ideas. And further, there were ample tutors in England who could further Minnie's studies and talk as much as she could tolerate about politics and philosophy. Yet it seemed a yawning void to embark on this penal adventure without her presence and encouragement.

All in all, it seemed not unreasonable to keep the family together for a year or two—it was certainly what my wife, Mary, wanted—and then let either or both the girls go home to my sister in England if that were then thought wise.

Later that day, in the afternoon, in the garden in front of the house we shared with the Franklins, I talked with Mary about our daughters. She thought that Norfolk Island would be useful for Catherine who seemed already preoccupied by the thought of marriage; it might well give her time to grow to a larger maturity before accepting the first faintly acceptable suitor—for she was a beautiful young girl and would attract many such suitors. Mary Ann was a different matter, Mary thought, but Mary also felt that she herself needed Mary Ann's help in what would likely be a difficult and lonely life on Norfolk Island, and that it was not asking too large a sacrifice for Mary Ann to devote the next year or two to the family's needs.

So, after reflection, we agreed that I would insist on Mary Ann accompanying us to Norfolk Island with the suggestion by Mary that after a year or two it might well be sensible for her to return to my sister in England. To both of them I proposed to stress the pleasures likely in Sydney while I made ready for my transfer to Norfolk Island.

When we spoke of this decision to the girls, Catherine seemed not displeased by the plan, while Mary Ann's response was curt and to the blunt effect that not yet being of age she could not properly oppose her parents, and then said no more.

The Old Testament presents some dreams as suitable for prediction of future events—bad seasons, poor crops, storms of toads and the like—and endows some seers with the capacity for their interpretation. Though not in doubt of my faith, I find such an idea wholly unlikely and am glad it does not much recur in the New Testament. For my part, I don't remember most of my dreams, though Mary and Mary Ann and Catherine have a lot to tell about theirs and do so freely.

Sometimes, if I am awakened suddenly by some outward event, the ship being engaged, a sudden change of the wind at sea, a call from a sentinel, I will have a memory of what I was dreaming about, but even that memory is shadowy and passes quickly.

Sailors at sea are quite superstitious about their dreams and claim immunity from taking risks in the riggings after some dream of tragedy, and they also extensively relate and no doubt imaginatively embroider their dreams of a sexual character. They certainly talk a lot about their dreams, real or later imagined. Some fellow officers have even told me of the colour and skin tonings of people in their dreams; for me, so far as I can recall, my snippets of dreams are in dull monochrome, and are entirely inconsequential—but not always.

Occasionally, very occasionally, my dream pattern varies, perhaps two or three times as I recall in my life. And it did on the night before we reached Sydney on our way to my new posting. I dreamt of a naked lady, rather of a girl, and a girl not at all unlike Mary Ann. Well, hardly a girl, more a young woman. And I was intimate with her; the bed-sheets and my memory both so testified. I cleaned up the former as best I could and thought about the latter, and thought and thought and worried and worried. How fragile loving relationships are! Did I really harbour such evil thoughts? Should I change my behaviour towards her? But that seemed ridiculous.

Was this a common experience of fathers of young woman daughters? I had no idea, and did not propose to ask anyone. I was certainly deeply fond of Mary Ann, but not unduly I thought, and there is no doubt that I would rather die than injure her. Was my affection excessive? I thought not; but the speed with which Mary and I had disposed of her desire to return to my sister in England gave me pause. At all events, nothing was now to be done; we had made our decision; we would stick to it.

They were called the "Heads," a misnomer to sailors, since they were the gates to the loveliest, safest anchorage in the world. The entire British fleet could be safe-harboured in this vast confluence of ocean and river, protected by the massive rock gates that shaped the entrance to Sydney town. The heads and the surrounding hills drew the sting from any weather these latitudes might produce. The heavy ordnance, perched on the heads, guarding the entrance to those waters, allowed entry to no hostile ship.

On the 23rd of February, 1840, I boarded the *Nautilus*, with a complement of over four hundred passengers, of whom three hundred were convicts, who had recently been transported from Ireland, and about one hundred soldiers and some of their families, including my wife, Mary, and our six children and myself. Leaving the heads we caught the easterly trade-winds, and the thousand-mile passage to the penal colony east–northeast of Sydney had begun. We reached Norfolk Island eleven days later and I was in charge thereafter of about 2,000 prisoners, of whom most were twice transported, doubly banished, once from England or Ireland, and then banished again for further offenses in New South Wales or Van Diemen's Land.

All Sydney had described them as incorrigible, the worst of the worst, but that was a superficiality. The three hundred on the *Nautilus* with me were merely the usual run of convicts—petty thieves, persistent poachers, political offenders, with a sprinkling of robbers and housebreakers and an occasional killer who had been thought not to merit the hangman's noose. Those awaiting me on the island were of sterner stuff, since they had continued the same or similar behaviour in the colonies, together with some military offenders for whom the lash was thought inadequate. But, all in all, I saw all 2,000 as presenting just the same problem to the penal authorities as I had seen around me in Van Dieman's Land and read about before then, a problem handled, it seemed to me, with inefficiency and cruelty, but capable of being largely replaced by a stern decency, a firm and fair administration, and the Marks System.

Nevertheless, I was well aware that my experience (even that period as a prisoner of war) did not fit me for the role I had sought, though I saw this as both an advantage and a disadvantage since I would not be bound by established, often injurious, routines.

With few exceptions, Norfolk Island would be populated only by prisoners and soldiers, the former outnumbering the latter by a factor of about five to one. The exceptions were my own family, and the dependents of a few of the soldiers who had accompanied their husbands or fathers to New South Wales and then on to Norfolk Island, and a handful of non-military prison administrators, also under my command, and their families. There would be no middle class, no artisans, no professional men other than those who served with the army or among the prisoners, all but a few of whom had come from poverty, through one or another form of stealing, to their present situation. It would be a two-tier society, prisoners and soldiers, and, as I had already learned on Van Diemen's Land, the latter had neither inclination nor training to serve as prison guards.

I was told that nobody was ever quite sure of the number of convicts on Norfolk Island. Death from the lash, disease, suicide, and despair visited regularly and made a tally difficult. Nor had I at this stage had a careful count made of the Irish prisoners who were with me on the *Nautilus*. Counting convicts mattered little enough on Norfolk Island. There are but two accessible landings for ships, one where we landed, known variously as Sydney Bay or Sandy Bay, the other, extremely hazardous, on the other side of the Island. For the rest, the sea beats on steeply rising cliffs, seriously impeding any attempt at escape by sea.

I am not beautiful. I am infelicitous in conversation. Though I am just seventeen, I hate to be treated as an empty-headed child. I try hard not to be caustic and direct with others, but I frequently fail. I find little interest in the transient and panting unrealities that shape my sister Catherine's emerging affairs of the heart, and those of most of the young ladies we have come to know in Hobart Town and Sydney. Only with Father do I find an openness of discussion, an ease of behaviour. I am "Minnie" to my mother, my sister, and brothers. To Father, from my earliest memories and until recently, I have also been "Minnie." Perhaps he now sees me as a grown woman. But our shared interests and habits of mind divide us from the rest of the family. He talks to me, and I to him, of his naval days, of the treatment of convicts, of the system of transportation, and of his geographic studies—the rest of the family find such topics boring and they do not trouble to conceal this reaction.

This has not made me a congenial member of the family. There is a resentment that expresses itself only in rare occasions of anger, mostly by my sister, Catherine; but I think the others feel it too. And I am both troubled by and rejoice in Father's ill-concealed, apparently larger affection for me. Perhaps that is wrong; perhaps there is no larger affection for me; he seems to love the entire family, but as an intellectually potential equal he certainly prefers me.

Nevertheless, privileged as I am, I find resentment in his willingness to give immediate precedence to any official or social duty over his attention to me or the rest of us in his family. Particularly in the past few weeks in Sydney he has devoted every waking minute to his plans for Norfolk Island and spoken hardly a word to us, except occasionally to solicit and receive my assistance in shaping a clean draft of one or another of his more confidential letters—my role as his back-up amanuensis. But yesterday he put all work aside; satisfied that he had done all he could, acquired all the supplies he needed, bought the books and musical instruments, persuaded all those who required persuasions to advance his plans for the Island settlement, and devoted the day and the evening to my

seventeenth birthday and the party given that night to cele-
brate it.

Apart from my family there had been no one I really cared
for at yesterday's party. In the few weeks we had been in Sydney I had met some young ladies of my own age and had been
introduced to a few young men in the army and to a few
civilian landowners. They were, all in all, a more lively bunch
than those in Hobart Town, but I still felt that my youth was
steadily being stolen from me. It seemed so long since we were
in relaxed and interesting society, and indeed it was a long
time. I had been fifteen when we embarked in Bristol on the
appalling *Fairlea* for that torturous journey from home. And
now, a day after my seventeenth birthday, we were sailing for
an even more distant banishment.

Our quarters on the *Nautilus* were, of course, far better than
the closet-like hole my sister, Catherine, and I had been packed
in on the *Fairlea*. Father was the ranking officer by far on the
Nautilus, both because he had been a Commander in the Navy
and because he was the new Commandant of Norfolk Island,
and some effort had been made to make us comfortable. I still
had to share a small cabin with Catherine. But now, though
two years younger than me, she has a sense of privacy which
makes close living more tolerable.

I had tried my best not to be morose at the party yesterday.
Mother and Father had demonstrated their love and consideration of me in many ways, and even my sister and four
young brothers had been affectionate, but I knew that in an
important way I was being badly treated.

What was there for me on Norfolk Island, even more remote from home than where we had been the past years? It
was not that marriage did not attract me, far from it; it was
rather that I found no one of interest among the soldiers and

settlers who had been sent or had brought themselves to this distant corner of the world—and I didn't think any such charmer would likely appear in these remote colonies. And now here I was suffering a yet further banishment to a penal colony devoted to the very worst convicts and to soldiers least required for military conflict, and therefore thought suitable to serve as prison warders and not much else—hardly the environs to find a husband for me, and certainly far removed from the romantic whirl of London society. My marriageable years, few even in London, were being stolen from me.

Yet it is so hard to be resentful of my parents. Mother always acts the peacemaker and finds much to be said on both sides of even the slightest disagreement, while Father lifts every hint of conflict to a level of principle and philosophic consideration, so that he still finds it hard to think of me as other than a precocious child, bound to him by ties of manifest love, whose intellectual development, for which he seems to hold himself responsible, is of more importance than anything other than her health.

Father could hardly be blamed for finding little time for us while we were in Sydney; there was much to be done before he could take charge of the penal hell that he, and no one else of his social standing, wished to govern. Why he should want it still amazed me. He had already succeeded in two careers: as a naval commander and as a geographer, being the first Professor of Geography at London University and the founding Executive Director of the Royal Geographic Society which had played such an important role in the heroic adventures of his erstwhile friend, Sir John Franklin. Why, with so much already achieved, he should have decided to come himself to the antipodean colonies, and to drag his family with him, was quite beyond my understanding—though it was clear to me

that he had become obsessed with his Marks System of Convict Discipline. (He always wrote it thus, as if it demanded to
be capitalised.) And now a yet further incomprehensible plan:
he believed he could take the most brutal convict settlement
in the young Queen's domain and turn it into what he called
a "moral hospital."

In Hobart Town, Father had first begun to develop his plans
for the governance of convict settlements, having been
prompted to this by his undertaking, before we left England,
to the Society for the Improvement of Prison Discipline. They
were, as I understand it, a segment of those who had worked
for the abolition of slavery in the colonies and in the New
World, who now likewise opposed what they saw as the brutality, akin to slavery, of our convict system. They had phrased
a list of sixty-seven questions about the convict regime in Van
Dieman's Land and had asked Father to reply to these questions after he had observed that system. He had agreed to do
so. In the family, I was the only one with whom he discussed
these matters. He talked to Mother of them, but she never
risked comment that hinted at disagreement, which is essential
to serious conversation. I, on the other hand, early saw this
new interest of his as a threat to our family's well-being, and
did not hesitate to quibble with and prod at his belief that
virtually all convicts could, by his system, be turned in time
from depravity to social conformity.

Father seemed to welcome my skepticism and, to my satisfaction, I noted some traces of my ideas creeping into the
documents he was regularly sending to officials and friends in
England.

My vague sense of the threat his ideas presented to our
family suddenly took shape in a letter from the Colonial Office
which had arrived one chill morning in Hobart. I had awak-

ened unusually early that morning and had decided to walk down to the wharf before breakfast. I saw a ship maneuvering just outside the entrance channel to the harbor, waiting for more favourable conditions to berth, while the ship's boat was being rowed ashore.

Mails from England came only sporadically to Hobart, and I knew that everyone would be anxious to learn the news from England as soon as we could. I should not have hurried. The mail proved to be a misery for me; it included the offer of the governance of Norfolk Island to my father, and directions to Sir John Franklin to facilitate our movement to that speck of an island, a thousand miles east of the coast of New South Wales.

To no avail, I pleaded with my parents to be allowed to return to England to live with Father's sister in Kent. Mother said she would need my help on Norfolk Island and cried at even the thought of our separation, while Father, somewhat dismissively, argued that it would be far better for my development to accompany the family for a year or two—but that I might then return to England if his duties on the island were to be of much longer duration. And so it was settled. And so I hated it; but I could not find it in my heart to be other than dutiful and loving toward my parents, though I knew they were sacrificing me, one to timidity, the other to what I could not precisely define.

I looked about me and these dark thoughts fled. What a superb, sunny day and what a beautiful scene! Leaning lightly to port, the *Nautilus* slid through the "Heads" out of Sydney's glowing harbour into the gently rolling Pacific.

Father strode about the deck, obviously delighted again to be at sea, and I must admit that the journey on the *Nautilus* was a delight, with steady cool breezes, sparkling days, and a slow rolling motion by night to ensure sound sleep.

Mother and the rest of her brood had endured periods of seasickness when we were speeding East in the turbulent latitudes of the roaring forties on the way from England, but sailing now in what we thought was the properly named Pacific produced no queasy feelings in anyone aboard. Even the three hundred convicts in their cruelly cramped quarters below decks seemed untroubled by the voyage.

Of course, I in no way mingled with them, but Father did. Daily he walked on the forward deck to which batches of the convicts were brought in groups each day for a taste of sun and exercise. I could not avoid taking pleasure in his obvious enjoyment of his new adventure, his happy determination to make his ideas live, his strong belief in the ultimate decency of everyone, his willingness to talk as man to man without affectation to everyone, high or low, aristocrat or twice-convicted felon alike. At times I would find him ingenuous, unreal, too trusting by far, and sometimes, in quieter moments when we were talking together, I would say so.

"You forget, Minnie, that I too have been a prisoner for over two years, a prisoner of war, admittedly, but it is much the same. It is not an easy condition. I think I know how they feel."

No, I had not forgotten. He had been a prisoner of war of the French after the surrender of the *Grasshopper* to the Dutch fleet; but prisoners of war seemed profoundly different to me from those convicted of criminal offenses. Father disagreed. Had he lacked education, lacked the support of a close family, endured hunger and desperation with little hope for the future, he could, he said, easily see himself as one with those now held below decks.

So, each sunny day, as we slid through the waters of this vast ocean, I would see him near the bow, moving and chatting, apparently easily and informally, to groups of convicts and to individuals among them.

Also each day, during our trip on the *Nautilus*, Father devoted an hour, sometimes more to me. It may be that he wanted to comfort me in my reluctance to go even further away from home, but I think he enjoyed the time we spent together nearly as much as I did. We called these meetings my "Latin lessons," so that neither my sister nor my brothers would be put out of countenance by the amount of time he gave to me. And much of what went on during these hours was indeed his trying to develop my rudimentary knowledge of Latin; but there were also many many asides on topics other than the language of early Rome.

Latin was not taught to young ladies at my London school. Latin was for boys. It presented too heavy a burden of memorising and intellectual effort for girls; everyone knew that. But Father didn't seem to understand. And what good would a knowledge of Latin be for a lady?

Father said that chance had played a big role in his career and that his knowledge of Latin was essential to giving him that chance. It had, he said, been of great practical use to him. His father, and later his guardian, when his father had died, were both successful men of the law and both had directed his education with the intention of his following their path to legal and then judicial practice. Latin was, of course, an integral part of such an education. But in 1803, aged sixteen, for reasons he did not offer to explain, he had gone to sea as a First Class Volunteer in the Royal Navy. Eight months later he was promoted to Midshipman. On Father's first voyage in Spanish waters, the captain of his ship encountered a problem of communication with Spanish monks. They spoke no English; no one on the ship spoke Spanish. Father was pressed into service as an interpreter by means of his knowledge of Latin, which the monks spoke fluently. The midshipman appointment followed. And this in turn led to his meeting with Lord Nelson. Yes, that's right, Lord Nelson.

When he first mentioned this I thought he was teasing me and I asked had he also met Lady Hamilton.

He blushed. Replied with a curt "No," but went on to describe how he had indeed met the great sailor. Well, "met" was perhaps not precisely the word.

Father had served in the West Indies on a ship commanded by Admiral Cochrane, when Nelson and the fleet were in pursuit of the French fleet. Nelson called a conference aboard his flagship, the *Victory*. Father was chosen as the midshipman to accompany Admiral Cochrane to this conference. And, as he later described it, this is what happened: "I was standing on her quarter-deck, when Lord Nelson came out of the cabin, with a large glass under his arm, and crossing to where I stood on the lee side, he said to me, 'Youngster, give me a shoulder,' and made a motion so to employ me; but, changing his mind, he turned up the poop ladder, and I never saw him afterwards."

I managed to get this Nelson story told to me at several of our Latin lessons. Innocent questions of its where, and how, and when, and how did you feel, produced a delightful mixture of modesty and boasting.

Father rarely boasted to me or to anyone else, but he did tell me that he had developed an idea that had not before been tried, and that had become a staple of near-polar navigation.

In 1815, then a twenty-eight-year-old ship's captain serving with the fleet off Quebec, he was ordered to sail ahead of the fleet to give intelligence to the Admiralty of the immediate return of the fleet to English waters in expectation of the war to be fought consequent on the escape of Bonaparte from Elba. The importance of this information to the Admiralty needed no underlining, and speed was imperative.

The further north the route taken, the swifter the passage; but also the more likely a deadly collision with an iceberg. How to strike a swift but safe balance?

He had thought, correctly, that the water proximate to an iceberg would be colder than the general temperature of the sea. Every few minutes throughout day and night he had a bucket in the bow drawn to test the water's temperature. Thus protected, risking a passage well to the north, he was able to reach England in nineteen days while the fleet took over thirty days to return home.

The closer I came to Father—and the voyage on the *Nautilus* fostered that closenesss—the less I understood why a man of his achievement and obvious intelligence should actually wish to run a convict settlement and would also willingly drag his family in his wake. Hesitantly, circumlocutiously I would ask him about his plans for Norfolk Island, receiving responses of no precision. He believed, he said, that the criminal in the dock and the judge on the bench were similar mixtures of good and evil, and that on Norfolk Island he would be able to prove that a rational system of convict administration would demonstrate that truth and the redeemability of all but a few convicts.

The outline of his scheme was this: Each convict would be allotted, on arrival at the prison, a number of "marks" according to the severity of his crime as measured by the length of his sentence. Each day thereafter, by virtue of good behaviour and diligent work, he would be awarded "marks" which would count by fixed accumulated amounts to ameliorate the severity of the conditions of his imprisonment and count toward his ultimate earlier release from prison, again by fixed accumulated amounts. Marks could, of course, be lost by disobedient or disrespectful or unseemly behavior and by sloth at, or neglect of, work.

The prisoner would, in effect, by his behavior and his labour determine the conditions and duration of his imprisonment. The details of this plan formed the "Marks System" which, Father believed, would turn current imprisonment practices from a brutal and useless severity into a forceful engine to achieve social conformity.

All this read exceedingly well, but it seemed unlikely to me that anyone would be taking an interest in whatever happened on Norfolk Island—they never had, and the place was certainly far enough out of sight to be out of mind. And I found unreal the thought of the typical soldier carefully recording each prisoner's daily good or bad behavior. My admiration for Father would turn to annoyance, and my mind would sink into self-pity. I sorely missed Lady Franklin who, in Hobart Town, had lent a kind ear to my troubles when no one else would.

I could not share my feelings with Mother or Catherine. Mother would find them disloyal and, even aboard the *Nautilus,* Catherine's main focus was on her appearance and whether one or two of the military officers aboard were taking sufficient notice of her. And the next day Father would again devote attention to me and my mindless adoration of him would return.

I regretted our imminent arrival at Norfolk Island. I knew Father would now have very much less time for me—I could hardly expect the Latin lessons to continue. And I feared the boredom and waste of my life that I anticipated in this remote corner of the Queen's domains.

We convicts were allowed above deck, in the foc'sle, for an hour a day, in groups of twenty. Instead of peering at us from the upper deck, like animals being exercised below, Maconochie had made it a habit to join us on our deck and talk informally to any who wished to talk with him. At first the convicts had crowded around him, not threateningly, but anxious for information. Soon it became clear that he knew little more than we did about Norfolk Island. He had heard the rumors of its being a brutal, hellish settlement, of excessive discipline and frequent scourging for the slightest offense; but so had we. He seemed more interested in our backgrounds, indeed in us, what skills we had, could we read and write, did we know a trade, could we farm, and so on.

"Your name, please," Maconochie said.

"Patrick Burke," I replied.

"Yes. I believe I have seen your record. Yes, I remember it now. I recall that you are one of those who claim to be innocent. Of what are you innocent?"

"Of many things," I replied, expecting at very least a rebuke for such disingenuous discourtesy, but he smiled slightly and reshaped his question. "Very well, I'll try to speak by the book. Of what crime were you convicted, though innocent you say, at the Clare Assizes, was it not, and sent here?"

"Sedition, Sir."

"And were you not seditious?"

"In general, I was; but not on the particular occasion which led to my conviction. I was trying to calm the mob, not lead them on, but that is not easy with an angry Irish mob. I was certainly there to listen if not to speak, and to advise if called upon, but I did indeed speak. I do not doubt that to English ears much of what was said, or shouted, was seditious. The court certainly thought so."

"So, all in all, you have no particular complaint. If not seditious on the occasion that led to your arrest, sedition was in the intention of your companions, and you knew it, and was probably in your intention too. So, if not seditious then, seditious earlier, and seditious in contemplation."

I could quibble no longer. It was my time for a rueful smile. Maconochie was obviously of a different stamp from others who ran prisons and it was not sensible for me to confront him in this flippant way. I found I didn't want to. This was the first occasion that I had had the chance to talk to him, and since I had come to respect his behavior on this voyage from Sydney to Norfolk Island I rather regretted my earlier evasive response to his inquiry.

"I know, Sir, that many aboard claim innocence of the crimes for which they have been transported. It happens that my claim is technically valid, but I am in no worse situation than many other convicts on this ship with you. It is not easy for the young, Irish, working man who has no work, to stay out of an English prison."

He made no direct reply but turned the conversation to my family and myself, teasing out the facts of my education and my work. I had been a printer and binder in my family's business, anticipating becoming its manager. But my resentment of English rule in Ireland, of their caring so little for our living conditions, of their hauteur and arrogance, had led me to my present situation. I said as much; he did not disagree. Rather, he asked if I had read any political philosophy and any studies on what he called "The Irish Question." I told him that my reading turned largely toward fiction, but that I had indeed read a few of the current pamphlets on Irish politics. He said he would like to talk to me further after we reached Norfolk Island, and then, most extraordinarily for a senior naval officer addressing a convict, excused himself and left the convict deck.

Mary and the children stayed on board with the rest of the ship's complement while I went ashore to arrange housing for my family, and whatever needed to be done to bring the Irish convicts ashore.

I had not met Major Charles Best, whom I was to replace as Superintendent of the Norfolk Island Penal Colony, and I rather dreaded the usual welcome at the military mess, soused in the rum, that was the votive substitute for both conversation and civility throughout the formal messes of the New South Wales Corps. I assumed he would be at the dockside when we berthed.

My first sight of my new posting was of a ramshackle pier poking out through a tropical downpour from a narrow bay, with a much larger beach to its right. A platoon of soldiers stood disconsolate on the pier. I moved to meet them as soon as the gangplank was down, my greatcoat heavy with rain. A major in charge of the small troop stepped forward to meet me, saluted, introduced himself as Major John Simmonds, and said, "Welcome to Norfolk Island, Sir" and held out to me an oilskin wrapped document.

I suggested we should all repair to the shed behind the pier on the shoreline. There we gathered, the soldiers drawn up at attention in three ranks, Simmonds, and me.

"The Commandant, Major Best, told me to present his compliments, to give you that letter, and to express his regret at his being unable to welcome you," Simmonds said.

I tried to put him at ease and suggested that the men be allowed to fall out and relax until the storm passed. I then read Major Best's letter.

It was hardly a welcome, rather a cry of relief at having escaped the Island. I was not to worry. Everything was in excellent order. Major Simmonds, who would meet me, was utterly reliable and knew everything necessary to run the colony. He, Charles Best, had had to depart a few days before I was expected to arrive since, unexpectedly, a supply boat with a contingent of new prisoners had arrived from Port Arthur and was heading immediately for Sydney. Such were the exigencies of shipping to and from the Island that he thought it his duty to take the first available passage back to his new posting which he had been led to believe, and here joy shone through his syntax, would be with the unit from which he had been seconded, and which was soon to be on its way home to England.

He had not, he wrote, found the governance of the convicts and the soldiers and their families a challenging job. It was largely a question of an unrelenting insistence on firm discipline and adequate punishment; but he had not enlisted with this type of service in mind and he did find the behavior of the prisoners bestial beyond tolerance, and this seemed even to have adverse effects on the soldiers.

With a final commendation of Major Simmonds, and another reference to the disciplinary needs of convicts and soldiers alike, he wished me well. He clearly sympathized with me in this posting. I had the sense that he would have liked to know what misfeasance of mine had led to the appointment of a naval captain as the governor of a desolate encampment of twice-transported convicts. He clearly knew nothing of my career and nothing of the additional convicts coming with me.

Best would have been astonished to learn that I had volunteered for this posting, that I had indeed pulled such strings as I could grasp in London to get it.

For years I had followed the debate between Jeremy Bentham and John Stuart Mill and Sir James Fitzjames Stephen about the governance of prison, about transportation and the purposes the prison and the penal colony might serve. I had come to know and esteem the work of Matthew Davenport Hill in saving lives otherwise utterly lost. I had seen the horror of the hulks and I had heard the fashionable talk about the unredeemability of the criminal classes. I had closely observed conditions in the Port Arthur colony. Philosophically, I had fallen under the influence of the Quakers, in particular of John Howard, and had come to believe, with him, that there is a spark in the breast of every man which if properly fanned and tended will lead him to an honorable life, and sometimes to a socially useful life. I had come firmly to believe in reformation of convicts by moral suasion, its stages encouraged and defined by a system of awarded merits and demerits.

I had published four articles in London which had attracted considerable attention, urging a prison regime in which the convict would be held in conditions of hardship and solitude for a period until by his behaviour he would earn a few privileges and some association with others in his situation, and so on, by stages of increasingly responsible work and increasing autonomy until by his industry and good behaviour he would merit trial release on parole, and ultimately complete freedom.

This staging system, which later became known as the "Marks System," seemed likely to me to fan that spark of decency I found in all men and would yet preserve the law's power over them for as long as necessary. When I phrased these ideas as a proposition—"the prisoner should hold the key to his own cell"—mockery knew no bounds. Few got beyond the phrase, which became the butt of jokes in the clubs.

Under the Marks System I had recommended in these papers, the prisoner would regularly be awarded marks for diligence and desirable behavior and would have marks deducted for disciplinary breaches and all forms of undesirable behaviour. These marks, his tally, would be known to the prisoner, and also the sum of marks he must attain to move to the next and less severe stage of his punishment; he would thus know where he stood in relation to his punishment. So, if he wished, and if he was capable of doing so, he could shorten the period of his punishment by fitting himself for conditional and then final release. He would, in effect, keep the key to his cell.

Among my fellow naval officers such views rang hollow, not to say absurd, a poor and effeminate substitute for the proved efficacy of the hangman, irons, and the lash. But I came from a family whose name was known. My active naval service had not been without widely published success. And a few did read and listen to my ideas.

I still do not know whether it was those few or the sardonic mockers who brought me to the Island. "Let him try giving those marks and keys to prisoners who have been transported to Sydney and Port Arthur and have there committed further crimes and have been further transported to Norfolk Island. Oh, yes: for good measure let us add to those at Norfolk Island the similar failures of the convict settlements in New South Wales and Van Diemen's Land. Nobody in those colonies will object."

I had argued that it was unfair to test my Marks System on the twice transported, on those who were seen as incorrigible, on those who had deeply and long experienced the hell that was current practice. The Colonial Office had not disagreed. I was ordered to confine my Marks System to those convicts who would be transported to Norfolk Island directly from England or Ireland, in effect, those accompanying me on the *Nautilus*. I was to keep them separate from the twice-transported convicts at present on the island; for them, I was to maintain the existing regime

Eventually the rain abated and a horse-drawn, clapboard cart came for Simmonds and me, the soldiers being placed under the orders of a lieutenant to make their way back to barracks.

I then saw my first batch of Norfolk Island convicts, a half dozen of them, apparently unsupervised, sodden wet from rough caps to muddy pantaloons. When they saw our approach, they fell to digging, to widen and deepen the ditch beside the road, or rather the track, on which we were travelling. As we drew close, they lined up in the ditch, took off their caps, which they held in their two hands in front of them, and cast their eyes down so as not to be seen even glancing in our direction.

I told the driver to stop. He looked to Simmonds, who nodded assent, but said to me that I should not stop here to talk to the men, unprotected as we were. I glanced at his side arm, which he was wearing since he was on formal duty, and decided to follow my instinct, which was to get down from the cart, approach the men, tell them my name and position, which I was sure they knew already, since prisons keep few secrets, and to ask for their names.

It was not a success. They were wet, cold, bewildered, and, I noted, scared. Names were mumbled, inaudibly so far as my ears could detect. Eyes remained downcast, except for brief upturnings as I addressed each man directly. All this changed when I came to the last man, even more unkempt than the others, standing somewhat apart from them, but in a similar subservient pose.

"What's your name, my man?" I asked.

His eyes widened, his head twisted back, he began to jig about, his arms waved, and jerky high-pitched laughter came from his crumpled mouth. Simmonds may well have been correct; I stepped back a pace or two. Simmonds hurried to my side.

One of the other prisoners called out, "He mean no harm, Sir. That's Bony. He be always like that."

I got back into the cart, bewildered by my first contact with my convict charges on the island—a miserable, depressed-looking lot, with apparently more than their share of lunacy.

A few minutes later I had my first view of Kingston, as the main convict settlement had been named. The prison compound dominated the settlement. Otherwise I found that the human habitations differed little from the description of them written six years earlier by the Reverend Ullathorne when he had visited the island: "a spacious quadrangle of buildings for the prisoners, the military barracks, and a series of offices in two ranges. A little further beyond, on a green mound of nature's beautiful making, rises the mansion of the Commandant,

with its barred windows, defensive cannon, and pacing sentry."
These words had comforted Mary, who feared for the safety
of our children, and they had stuck in my mind.

I found the Commandant's residence to be a substantial
single-story building of porous limestone with rough cast on
the outside to keep out the damp sea air. It was in excellent
condition, scrubbed clean, and comfortably, though sparsely,
furnished for our reception. The house commanded a view
over the entire Kingston settlement, being built on a mound
gently sloped to the level ground of the settlement. Officers'
houses, the military barracks, the prison, the officers' gardens,
all were clearly visible from my new front door.

I arranged for assistance in bringing my family from the
Nautilus to our quarters, and returned immediately to the ship
to oversee their arrival at our new home, leaving Major Simmonds to make appropriate arrangements to disembark and
contain the Irish convicts. I was informed that they would be
held in the stockade at Longridge, the other settlement on the
island. I advised him that I wanted a general parade to be
arranged for all prisoners two days hence—the doubly transported and these recent arrivals—which I would address.

In one of our so-called "Latin lessons," Father had described
Norfolk Island to me as an island some eight miles long and
five miles wide, blessed with an oceanic, clement climate, and
lush with rich vegetation. At first sight it belied this reputation;
on the day of our arrival it looked a soggy mess.

Mother, Catherine, and I were anxious to get off the ship
and into our new home. Eventually a cart-like vehicle, covered
by an ill-fitting tarpaulin, and drawn by two heavy, mud-

bespattered horses, came for us and our personal luggage. The tarpaulin kept out some of the rain, but the rest blew in. The horses labored up the substantial incline from the beach to the small hill on the top of which our new home sat.

It was not a happy arrival. What was called "Government House" was large enough for our family, with sufficient public rooms, but it was furnished more like a barracks than a home, and the iron-barred windows and the two small cannon at the entrance were far from reassuring.

I suppose it was silly of me to expect a comfortable home to await us—as it always had in my past. The previous Commandant had taken his own furniture away with him, and we had brought ours with us on the *Nautilus*, so that army chairs, tables, and cots were a reasonable interim provision. And a substantial fire had been lit in the front hall to welcome us, around which the family, other than Father, huddled to dry.

A few soldiers were milling about to help us, and I noticed that the kitchen was manned by two convicts under the eye of a corporal, the convicts starkly distinct in their white canvas pants and shirts marked with black, broad arrows. They seemed to get on quite well with the corporal and the other soldiers, and my brothers soon found their way to the kitchen and an easy though courteous camaraderie.

It was a strange world so different from Sydney and Hobart Town, so very very different from our home in London. Mother was wonderful: busy, commanding, and encouraging. Catherine and I and the four boys found pleasure in helping her and reassuring one another that we would soon enjoy this strange new world.

The house was circumscribed by a broad, tin-roofed verandah, the iron-barred windows and doors set threateningly behind it.

Looking back toward the *Nautilus* I could see the long, low wall of the prison, and beyond it the sheds near the jetty where we had landed. Not far out to sea, two small islands were visible, one hardly more than a large rock protruding from the waves. As the day calmed, the view became not unpleasant. The prison was to a degree shielded from sight by rows of tall, straight pines and off to my right, parallel to the prison, were a few neat, two-storey houses of senior staff and then the taller, typical square military barracks. And behind, as one looked inland, gently rolling hills and tall grasses dotted with pines. All in all, raw but not unseemly surroundings.

It was an unlikely world. There could hardly be anything here of interest or help to me, other than within the resources of our own family. Perhaps I could improve my painting; I doubted it since it was tuition and criticism I needed, not practice. Perhaps I could improve my ability on the piano, for a piano had been left or contributed by a previous occupant, but there was the same difficulty that what I really needed was tuition and criticism. Perhaps I could help Father in his work, but I doubted that he would let me, other than as someone to talk to about what he was doing and what he planned, and to act as an occasional amanuensis for correspondence of which he wished the usual bureaucratic and military channels to be ignorant—the prevailing attitude to women was too rigidly negative for any more public role. I suppose I could help with the school, for there were children of some of the army and my younger brothers needing schooling, but it was a duty I had never enjoyed. No question about it, for me it would be a banishment from most everything that interested me so far in my life. Depressed and anxious, I went to bed early that first night on an army cot in a room for the time being shared with Catherine—and slept soundly.

A considerable number of soldiers, well armed, came down to the pier to escort us convicts from the ship to our stockade. We were a bedraggled lot. We had been on the *Nautilus* for over two months. We stank. We had been cramped together endlessly, it seemed. One hour a day topside, and even then crowded on a small deck, is not enough to fill the lungs nor blow away the bugs, and trying to clean oneself and one's clothes below decks in seawater does not make for a smart appearance. We had, of course, been moored in Sydney harbour for a few days, while we unloaded some free settlers and those convicts who had suffered from scurvy and other disease on the long journey from Portsmouth, and in those few days we had cleaned ourselves up as best we could, but we remained, even for convicts, a filthy and bedraggled lot.

I had tried to exercise every day on the ship but I found the march to the stockade at Longridge, a distance of about a mile and a half from the *Nautilus*, quite exhausting—sea legs acquired from months in crowded quarters were no preparation for rough ground and a herded walk.

At Longridge we were ordered to single cells, one man to a cell. The cells were of wood, with iron bolts and locking devices, and a dirt floor. Two rough rugs were folded in the corner of each cell as bedding and coverage by night. There was also an issue of clothes and a new pair of boots.

We were permitted to keep the boots we came in, if we wanted to; but we were ordered to throw all our old clothes out of the cells where, I assumed, they would be collected and washed or burnt—but they were no longer ours, that was made quite clear. As the cells had been filled up at random, the first cell for the first man in the stockade, and so on, I was surprised that my issue of clothing and boots fitted me so well; I am of middle height and apparently ordinary proportions, but my fellow convicts came in a wide variety of shapes and sizes—what of them?

So that was why so much attention had been given on the journey out to discovering who were the bootmakers among us, who could sew, and who had any tailoring experience. We had all been issued a jacket of white duck canvas, a waistcoat, two check shirts, one pair of drawers, three pairs of trousers of white duck canvas, three pairs of socks, one pair of boots, and a cap. The jacket and trousers were also marked by a few broad, black arrowheads to symbolise our convict status.

I wondered why there had been no inquiry as to who among us had any experience as cooks. I soon discovered why. Our first meal arrived. It was a rather thick gruel made of maize and some other mysterious ingredients, together with a piece of salted meat which determination could make chewable. We were told that in due time we would be able to arrange for some cooking of the meat and some other additions to our diet, but for the time being that was what we would get, together with water to be drunk from a bucket shared with others.

To my utter surprise I did not feel downcast by my situation. I calculated that I was antipodean to my home and family in County Clare—any move, east or west, would bring me closer to home. I could hardly be more banished while I lived. The Island itself seemed beautiful, though I had seen only a small part of it, the hills graceful, the pines tall, shapely, and plentiful, and when the rain had lifted the weather was warm, clear, and crisp. And I had no sense of guilt in my banishment; I had done nothing of which I need be ashamed. It was true that my companions in adversity were in the main undignified and ill educated, dirty and illiterate, but in the cramped hardships of the sweaty journey to Sydney, and on to the island, I had witnessed some degree of cooperation between many of them, some hints of mutual kindness.

The situation of the tailors and bootmakers among them gave me pleasure. If the larger men were to walk at all, the bootmakers would have to adjust the boots to their feet; if the taller and shorter, slimmer, and fatter, among us were not to look grossly incongruous, the tailors would have to go to work. And if the tailors and bootmakers had what were in effect saleable skills, so did I. My skills, I realised, the product of my decent schooling, far exceeded those of all but a few of my fellow convicts and, I surmised with confidence, all but a few of the soldiers who had shepherded us to the Longridge stockade. My fourteen-year sentence would not pass swiftly, I knew, but there had been much talk of tickets-of-leave, of clemency for those who could serve the colony, of the colonial need for shopkeepers and clerks; there was a void to fill between the army and the convicts on Norfolk Island and in New South Wales, which might be turned to my advantage. My family ties were not inconsiderable, but my life might well be better shaped in Sydney, which seemed a glorious place as we were held at anchor in its harbour, and even here on Norfolk Island there seemed at least a possibility that I could materially improve my conditions—at any rate, they couldn't get much worse. In short, for reasons that escaped me, I did not feel as depressed as my situation suggested.

They filled the hollow square of the prison, nearly 2,000 of them, filthily dressed in soiled duck pants, jackets, and caps, shod in black boots. Eyes downcast, talking, if at all, through nearly closed mouths without perceptible lip movement. Those from the *Nautilus* had been paraded somewhat apart from the doubly transported, and they held themselves less abjectly than the others, but still abject enough—too abject for my taste.

Words did not come easily. I had often, with moderate success, addressed parades of sailors and soldiers, in war and in peace; but never had I felt so inept. The day was shiny, the sun warm, the breeze brisk; but my heart was heavy indeed. I regretted calling them together; I should, I supposed, have tried to address the two groups separately. I might bring hope and comfort to the recent Irish contingent, but I had little to offer to the doubly convicted, except an effort at a fair administration. And then the stench began to bother me.

I found myself thinking of how these men lived, crowded together in bug-ridden cells and dormitories, fed in a shed which could hold about half their number, the rest eating outside proximate to a stinking communal privy, their food lifted to their mouths by their fingers, since knives and forks were prohibited, lacking sufficient water regularly to wash themselves or their drab clothes, and compelled to try to clean themselves without paper after defecation. And, lurking behind these miseries, lay solitary confinement, irons, the lash, and the scourger.

But these were not the thoughts I should be thinking as I stood ready to address my charges. I braced to begin; let me start about myself and then move on to my plans for them.

I am not one to whom a turn of phrase comes spontaneously and today was no exception. It was a dull and repetitious speech. It went on and on, I am told, for some thirty minutes; it should have been much shorter. It was a failure; but it may

have smoothed the path to later talks with groups of the convicts and individuals among them.

I started by telling the men to sit on the ground, and this
they did though the armed soldiers surrounding them stood
as a continuing threat. I gave my name and naval appointment.
I told them that I had come from Van Diemen's Land where
I had been secretary to the Governor, Sir John Franklin. I told
them I had become interested in the governance of convicts
and was of the view that fair and firm discipline should replace
random severity. I gave them an outline of the Marks System
and said that I would soon publish details of what it might
mean to them. Reluctantly, I added that there was difficulty
in applying this system to the doubly transported among them;
but I stressed that I would try my best, if they demonstrated
their fitness for release, to help them to an earlier freedom
than they had anticipated, both on and off the island. I had
no peroration; I just stopped.

There was little reaction to what I had said; I do not know
what I hoped for.

A few days in my cell at the Longridge stockade cured my
earlier mindless contentment. Hour after hour alone in the
cell, with only brief spells out for grimly unchanging meals,
eaten without benefit of knife, fork, or spoon, and, above all,
nothing to do, nothing whatsoever, hour after hour after
hour, taught me a meaning of boredom I had never before
experienced.

I contemplated escape. The wooden cells and iron locks
provided a far from difficult obstacle; but where to go once at
large? Escape *on* the island seemed absurd; escape *from* the

island would require months, perhaps years of difficult planning, a ship to be seized or built and hidden (and I could not imagine how that could be done) and the cooperation of many hands and minds—an impossibility at this stage, and probably always, since we were a thousand miles from our nearest neighbour, and that neighbour another penal colony.

The guards said they thought it would soon change; time would not hang so heavy; soon we would be put to work. But for the time being our keepers' every energy was devoted to getting the stockade moderately clean and tidy for Maconochie's inspection. It really didn't matter if we weren't clean and tidy.

Maconochie came to Longridge on the fifth day after his address to all of us in the yard at Kingston prison. We were told to stand in front of our cells, at ease, legs apart, our hands clasped behind our backs, and not to speak unless spoken to.

On the journey out I had seen men flogged and had no intention of risking that for myself. I certainly would try to do what I was told in these matters of discipline, of no importance in themselves, but apparently of immense importance to our jailers.

Maconochie, dressed informally in riding pants and a loose shirt, walked through the entire stockade and past all of us standing in front of our cells. He stopped to speak occasionally and briefly with a prisoner or a guard. To my considerable surprise, when he came to my cell, he nodded his recognition of me and said a courteous "Good morning, Mr. Burke," to which I made the appropriate reply, "Good morning, Sir." He did not speak further to me but turned to the officer accompanying him on his inspection and said, loud enough for me to hear, "Please arrange for this prisoner to be brought to see me when we have completed our rounds."

About half an hour later, I was taken to a small office in the front of the stockade, furnished with a rough table and three chairs, and told to wait there, a guard being placed outside the door. Soon Captain Maconochie arrived, alone. He reminded me of our talk on the *Nautilus*, of which I needed no reminding, and said that he had been thinking about my situation. He had, he said, "brought a small library and a collection of musical scores and musical instruments with him," and he suggested I might be interested to serve as librarian to the island and also to look after the musical equipment.

My strange euphoria when I first came to Longridge suddenly seemed justified. Surely, as librarian to the Island I would have as easy a life and as good prospects for release before the expiration of my sentence as I could hope for. I tried not to be overenthusiastic in my acceptance of this opportunity, but I'm sure I failed.

"We'll have a small hut built for the library and for you."

Within a week I had made up my mind. They could not be expected to work together daily in the quarry and mines and yards of the island and yet be subject to a profoundly different disciplinary regime, and profoundly different opportunities for release. In the space and conditions of this island, it was impossible to test the Marks System on one batch of prisoners and not on the others. Nor could the doubly transported prisoners be banished further or returned to New South Wales or to Van Diemen's Land; for that I lacked authority. My orders not to treat all alike had either to be disobeyed or the Marks System could not be tested. I chose the former alternative and wrote a letter to Governor Gipps in New South Wales, my immediate superior in this endeavor, explaining my reasons to him.

I did not wait for a reply. I got ahead with the business of trying to turn the hell that was Norfolk Island into a decent penal colony from which hope had not been banished, not only for the "new hands," as they came to be called, who had sailed with me on the *Nautilus*, but also for the "old hands," the many times convicted and twice transported, who were seen as incorrigible.

The new hands would continue to be held at Longridge, the old hands remained at the overcrowded, stinking prison at Kingston, but I decided that gradually the same opportunities to earn better conditions, an island ticket-of-leave, and ultimately freedom, would be available to them all, so far as I could arrange it.

And I took another early decision—Major Simmonds said a premature decision—about life for convicts on the island. If I was to make an impact with my Marks System on a deeply ingrained and brutal regime, I should give prompt talisman of the direction of my intentions. I ordered the cessation of any work by chain gangs.

Chain gangs came to the world, I suspected, with the first strong metal chain. They were not invented in New South Wales, but chain gangs came to an evil flowering in the penal colonies of New South Wales and Van Diemen's Land, and they had spread luxuriantly on Norfolk Island.

I had seen groups of prisoners chained together going out to work from the prison at Port Arthur, and I had read about them in the evidence given in parliament to the Select Committee on Transportation. That committee reported that in 1837 there were in New South Wales about 1,000 convicts in chain gangs, and about seven hundred in Van Diemen's Land.

Sir Richard Bourke had told the Committee "that the condition of the convicts in the chain-gangs was one of great pri-
vation and unhappiness." That was a prodigious understate-
ment, for he had gone on to describe men locked up from
sunset to sunrise in caravans or boxes holding between twenty
to twenty-eight men in which, for lack of room, they could
not all stand up or sit down at the same time (except with
their legs at right angles to their bodies) and, which, in some
instances "do not allow more than 18 inches in width for each
individual to lie upon bare boards."

I had seen and smelt such conditions for myself—an overwhelming stench of sweat and dirt, urine and feces, with desperation and hatred on the faces of the men.

They worked each day under a strict military guard and, as
Sir Richard reported to the Select Committee, "were liable to
suffer flagellation for trifling offences, such as an exhibition of
obstinacy, insolence, and the like. Being in chains, discipline
is more easily preserved among them, and escape more easily
prevented than among the road-parties out of chains."

Another witness before the same Select Committee, Colonel
Breton, who had commanded a regiment in New South Wales,
told the committee that chain gangs also produced "the
greatest demoralization among the troops," pointing out that
many of the soldiers came from the same circumstances and
villages in England and Ireland as the convicts and sometimes
found themselves guarding their fathers, brothers, and other
relatives among the chained convicts. And this combined with
the ready availablility of rum to the troops, and its consequent
seepage to some convicts, did indeed demoralize many of the
kept and the keepers. He, himself, said Colonel Breton, had
had to sentence sixteen soldiers to Norfolk Island for being
drunk on duty.

Thus, from my own observations and from the reports of others I respected, it seemed to me obvious that on Norfolk Island, since escape from the island was a near impossibility, chain gangs should not be tolerated. And so it was, before the end of the month of my arrival.

Men in punishment status, being moved from place to place, might have to be put in chains, but never a chain gang as a working team. If bullocks were lacking, teams of convicts might have to pull the plough, but not chained together.

Major Simmonds remonstrated with me about this, pointing out the danger of a group of unchained convicts, working away from central control and the mass of their guards, being able, easily enough were they so minded, to overpower their overseers, but, finding me adamant, saw that my order was promptly implemented.

We both knew that absent locks and firearms, a settlement like ours, and indeed nearly every prison, has to run with the consent of the convicts, that consent being coerced by ultimate power but not by immediate power. Certainly, when working away from the prison, immediate power lay with the prisoners.

It is one thing to talk and write about the governance of convict prisons and to draft papers for a Select Committee of the House of Commons; quite another to define in detail the rules and procedures for a penal colony, and to tell the prisoners and military staff alike precisely what those rules and procedures are to be. When I shared the principles of my Marks System with my peers I felt secure; confidence fled when I had to direct my island charges in detail. I had never worked in and certainly had never before directed any element of a convict settlement.

Nevertheless, I prepared a description of the Marks System

as simply as I could and had it posted in the prisons, barracks, stockades, and workplaces throughout the island. I wrote that the previous regulations would stay in force except where they were contradicted by those that I then published. This left a great deal of room for discretion, so I reserved to myself the exercise of that discretion where conflict was alleged.

Apart from explaining the role of marks to measure progress or regression for each convict, the plan was to keep in place existing regulations, but to interpret them and see that they were interpreted with less thoughtless severity. In particular, I announced that I would review all recommendations for flogging as a disciplinary sanction. One idea, which I did not risk at this early stage, was that ultimately I would arrange for ticket-of-leave convicts to serve as a jury in less serious criminal cases. If that proceeded as well as I hoped it might, I would then prudently expand it to more serious cases.

Major Simmonds was a great help on the minutiae of my fledgling regulations. He disagreed with many of them, but did not hesitate to help me draft them to apply in the real context of convict life.

Major Best's letter greeting me on my arrival had urged the virtues of Major Simmonds—the message was, in effect, rely on him and all will be well. He can hardly have predicted just how useful Simmonds proved to be, not as a reliable second-in-command who would take every decision for me, which is what Best probably had in mind, but as an effective and in-formed foil for my ideas. He did not conceal his disagreement with much I asked of him, but he nevertheless carried out my orders with subtlety and diligence, varying them only so far as necessary when his experience and knowledge so dictated, and then always promptly explaining to me what he had done. He had little confidence in the broad sweep of my plans, and told me so, regarding my faith in the reformability of prisoners, other than by the fear of severe punishment, as kindly but wrongheaded, and likely to lead us both into very hot water. But he never opposed me in action, only in words, and then only in words between us.

In the result, with his help, it became possible to launch my regime in some amplitude on the Island.

In our last few months in Port Arthur, Father had been busy at his desk writing to friends and acquaintances in England and Sydney soliciting an appointment appropiate to his station. I knew he found this somewhat humiliating, but it was obvious to Mother and to me that the situation in Van Diemen's Land was becoming impossibly difficult both for him and Sir John Franklin. They remained outwardly on polite terms, but the very politeness, almost exaggerated politeness, did not at all conceal my Father's resentment of Sir John's acceptance of the criticism he daily received from that faction of petty bureaucrats, hostile to my Father, who enjoyed the Governor's favour. So Father had little choice but to throw out more and more tentacles of enquiry.

Father kept copies of his correspondence, or rather he would edit his first draft and then write a clean draft from it for postage, so that he would have what amounted to a copy. A few times in Port Arthur he had been satisfied with his first draft and had asked me, as a favour, to make a copy for him to keep. Of course, it was a joy to be so treated, to be even further taken into his confidence than he had in his talks with me about the treatment of convicts and his ideas of how they should be treated—the emergence of his Marks System. Not many sixteen-year-old daughters were allowed to be of help to their fathers, and I took pride in it.

Mother and Catherine, of course, disapproved, but did not think it a serious fault on his or my part. By contrast, Lady Franklin expressed to me her pleasure that I could be of such use to my Father. I always found her a support and had increasingly confided to her my misery in what I saw as my banished and useless situation.

Soon after he was offered the appointment to Norfolk Island, my role began to change. Would I mind doing a first draft of a note to whoever it was so that he could get ahead with other things? He would look at my draught that evening and copy it out, or edit it for me to copy, and he would have a letter to send and what amounted to a copy to keep. Would I mind? Certainly not. And then in Sydney, where he was extremely busy, several of my drafts became his letters, often with few or no amendments, and I would make a clean copy for him to sign.

It was not that he lacked secretarial assistance within the army or the bureaucracy, but rather that he was now turning his ranging personal and private contacts into aides in his plans for his work on Norfolk Island and into pockets or pressure for things he needed for Norfolk Island but did not have the authority or the time to get through government sources, so that much of the correspondence with which I helped was of a quite solicitous and personal nature.

On the *Nautilus* to Norfolk Island my role of unofficial private secretary ceased—Father took such delight in the trip, in his family, and in his impending new job that he felt no need to write to anyone. But gradually on Norfolk Island he came again to rely on me for communications that lay outside his official and open role, which could be handled by the army secretaries. It added a quality to my life that substantially lessened my sense of isolation. There was not much for me to do in the school—five half days of teaching each week, teaching some reading, writing and counting to a not particularly bright group of young, army children—thankfully my brothers being taught by other than their elder sister, which would not have been at all easy—and the rest of the seven days being filled with . . . what? So I did my earnest best to satisfy Father in every letter I drafted or wrote for him so that he came more and more to treat me as his personal private secretary.

I now remember that he did ask me to copy one letter he wrote on the *Nautilus* for that ship to take back to Sydney. A letter to Sir George Gipps, the Governor of New South Wales. In it he had stressed how difficult it would be for him to make his Marks System work if he could not with some confidence rely on his own judgment and that of his Norfolk Island staff as to when a given convict might be suitable for return to Sydney on a ticket-of-leave. If he did not have some leeway here, some reasonable regularity in the acceptance of his recommendations for such trial releases, he did not see how he could fairly test his system. He could, of course, give island tickets-of-leave without consulting anyone, allowing the convict a large degree of freedom on the island, but the aim of most prisoners was to return to Sydney and perhaps thence in time to England or Ireland and this was the lure that could make his system work if steps to those increasing degrees of freedom were earned, observed, and had some reasonably predictable outcome. He was not asking for the authority for such trial releases from the Island to be delegated to him. He knew it was Sir George who must approve if it were to be made before the prisoner's court imposed term had elapsed, and likewise by the English authorities if it were a larger return; he was rather asking for a general understanding in the difficulty of his situation if his recommendations were not taken very seriously.

I thought it a fine letter, but even I could see that it would be impossible for Sir George Gipps to give other than a vague and general reply of goodwill to it. These were ultimately political questions, turning on the likely attitude of people in Sydney and London to the return of a particular convict, no matter what his conduct on Norfolk Island or contribution to life on Norfolk Island might have been. Even I, at this early stage, could see that it presented a very serious obstacle to my Father's plans.

Maconochie had spoken of a hut being built for the library and me; but this did not happen. Instead, soon after he had made this suggestion, I was moved to a small office in Kingston prison and told to turn it into both the library and my cell.

The office was well situated to serve as a library. It was near the administrative offices, but not a part of them. Somewhat half-heartedly I remonstrated that the room was too small, that the books and musical scores and instruments (which I also found stored there) would fill the space entirely, and was told that if that proved to be so a further, larger room, next door to the office, would also be made available.

In one respect the move from Longridge to this office troubled me. For living purposes, even with the books and other paraphernalia, it far exceeded the comfort of my cell at the Longridge stockade; but it struck me that my fellow prisoners there, and certainly the old hands here at Kingston, might well see me as having allied myself with the prison authorities, as being a traitor to my kind, and might look unkindly, and act more unkindly, on what they would see as my betrayal. Jealousy would fuel their annoyance.

There was not much I could do about this. It seemed to me that my only course to turn aside these sentiments was swiftly to make myself useful to the prisoners at both prisons, so useful that they would be less likely to see me as a spy for the authorities. Hence I diligently tried to help the "readers" Maconochie had introduced into the evenings in both prisons to try better to fill those depressing pre-sleep hours, and solicitously, and without hint of affectation, I tried to interest as many even vaguely literate prisoners as possible in reading, by lending them books from my relatively meager stock suited to their capacities—and followed this up by regular inquiries how the books were serving them.

Just as the bootmakers and tailors had improved their lot among their fellow prisoners by service to them, so would I. Without asking permission, I cut the door to my "cell" in half, so that the lower half could remain shut while the upper half opened outwards. Above the door, I put a sign "MACONOCHIE'S BOOK BUREAU." I made a living nest for myself in the far corner of the room, sheltered by rough bookshelves. It did not take me long to complete these tasks; I found I enjoyed them.

And then Maconochie came again with a further direction, which he phrased as a request: "The army has a printing press. Major Simmonds has agreed that we can put it under your control, other than when army orders are to be printed. If you can fit it in, it will be brought here. And from time to time I will give you material to print."

I was, I think, one of the first of the "new" convicts released to a conditional freedom on the island, what Maconochie called an "island ticket-of-leave." Many followed me to their own gardens and huts, well away from the two prisons, with their own goats and pigs and crops, until in time what had seemed merely a place of prisons became a settlement of convicts.

Many lived alone, were supplied by the prisons with maize and potatoes and salted meat, fended for themselves to improve their conditions, but some formed small groups of two or three "ticket-of-leave men," and became indistiguishable, except by dress, from many of the soldiers who were also allowed to have their own quarters. These, of course, differed also in that some of the soldiers were accompanied by their wives and children.

It became my daily habit to walk alone to the prisons, to the hospital, the crank mill, the lumber yard, the tailor shop, the bootmakers, the farmyard, the vegetable gardens, and further afield to the quarry and the outlying agricultural and road works. Everywhere I went, I tried to talk to the prisoners and to their guards, individually or in small groups. Major Simmonds objected strongly to this. He made the point that there were many among the prisoners who would gladly welcome the hangman as a means of escape from the endless misery and cruelty of their lives, and execution would certainly meet the man who killed me. I was, he said, entirely unprotected. To drive home the point, he insisted that his view on this should be formally recorded since he was reluctant to risk being thought to have failed in his duty should I be killed.

As I read the records of disciplinary hearings, of summary and severe punishments for minor discourtesies, and of hundreds of lashes for what was thought to be disobedience or insolence, I came to understand the force of his argument. Nevertheless, if I was to test my ideas about the punishment of convicts, it was necessary that I should be able to speak freely with them and that could be done, it seemed to me, only if I was not accompanied by a guard.

And there was another reason why I thought myself in no great danger, alone and unarmed among the convicts. I had come to believe that a considerable number of the convicts, by no means all but a goodly number, already knew that I was their best hope of minimizing the pains of their penal sentences. I had reduced the amount of needless and excessive punishment they had previously suffered. I had held out the hope of an earlier release from the island. They may have little confidence in the reality of these expectations, but I was their best hope, and they would, I thought, not lightly see those expectations dashed by the more violent and uncontrolled amongst them.

This was not just a vain hope of mine; I had seen it to a degree in my wanderings on the Island. I had observed prisoners keeping a wary eye on me, close enough to be of assistance, moving to keep a hostile prisoner away from me, ready to protect me should that be necessary. I was sure this was not imagination, but I understood that it was no expression of affection—I was their insulation from brutality and the prolongation of their suffering. Clearly the right-minded amongst them would be my protectors should that be necessary. And so I continued my frequent, solitary walks and rides all over the island.

Possibly I underrate the prisoners' motives in ensuring my safety. Given their life experiences and their current situation, many of them did possibly generate some degree of affection for anyone who was civil to them and appeared to have their interests in mind. At any rate, it gave me pleasure to believe so.

Norfolk Island was physically the right size for my purposes. Shaped rather like a fat dumbbell, it was nearly eight miles in length and about five miles broad. Tall pine trees, later widely known as Norfolk Pines, still dominated the landscape, as they did when Captain James Cook discovered the island. Cook noted the excellence of the pines for masts, yards, and other wooden fittings for His Majesty's ships; he also made mention of the extent of flax, necessary for rope and sails, which was growing wild in open areas between the forests of pines. Since the climate was equable and the soil fertile, Cook wrote that maize would likely be a fine crop—which it proved to be.

Norfolk Island lay uninhabited and uncultivated until 1788. Thereafter, several crops had flourished. Maize and potatoes grew plentifully and, added to salted meat, now formed the staple diet of the convicts. Corn and tobacco were also grown, but the latter caused problems for the convicts and their guards since the convicts were prohibited tobacco.

The two settlements, one at Kingston, the other at Longridge, housed the bulk of my colony, with a prison at each. At each some houses had been built for the military commissioned and non-commissioned officers. Some soldiers had also built small houses well away from the two settlements, had cultivated land around them, and had run some livestock. There were also, scattered over the island, a few huts for convicts who were allowed a ticket-of-leave, and they too had done their best to develop the land. I found these a benefit to my regime and determined to increase their number to take pressure off the two prisons and to form an integral part of my Marks System.

The island, small though it is, stands high from the sea, at an average elevation of over 350 feet and with two peaks, Mt. Pitt and Mt. Bates, each exceeding a thousand feet.

Not every day, but usually four or five times a week, I would ride or walk over my island. I came to think of these tours as my "rounds," like a doctor making the daily rounds of his patients in hospital. The comparison pleased me; my island would become a moral hospital. On these rounds I would talk with some of those in my charge, prisoner and freeman alike, and I did not hesitate to try to explain the regulations I had published to set out how my Marks System would apply.

It was not only the personal mail with which I helped my Father that began to trouble me about one aspect of punishment of the prisoners on Norfolk Island, but also the newspapers from Sydney. Much was made of the increase of some abominable crime among the prisoners which had, it was said, increased during Father's administration of the settlement. I assumed all this was referring to some sort of beating or fighting or extortion or theft among the convicts. I asked Father about it. He was evasive, but said that nothing of what was suggested was true; indeed, crime among the prisoners had decreased since his arrival and he had arranged readers and lights in the evenings in the dormitories to help in this. He was obviously not anxious to pursue the matter further and I let it drop. But it kept cropping up in correspondence and then I heard from the one convict with whom I had developed a somewhat open conversation, Patrick Burke in the library, that a friend of his had been flogged that morning and that was why he had been abrupt, he feared, less than courteous, when I spoke to him about some book or another.

I asked my Father about the flogging. "What had he done?" Again Father seeemed evasive and embarrassed. He would try to tell me. Did I understand about how babies were born? Of course, I did—I had a younger sister and four younger brothers and I had been with Mother just up to the actual birth of the younger boys. Did I understand how men and women fell in love with one another, wanted to live with one another, wanted to marry? Of course, I did—I had observed Mother and him together for all my eighteen years. Well then, he said, when men are alone for a long time without any women they sometimes, at least some of them, seem to fall in love with one another. That's what the papers and a few letters you see are written about. Do you understand? I said I did, but really I didn't. He, though, obviously had had enough of the topic and returned to his newspaper.

Nevertheless a few minutes later I did say: "Why flog a man for that?" To which he replied that it could not be allowed, not in the navy, the army, and certainly not in a prison, with which I had to be content, and would I please get on with the letter I was drafting for him.

I did not trouble him further with that subject, even though I had little understanding of what he had been talking about, though I began to reflect on it with increasing though imprecise perturbation. And what about me, in the reverse situation, with all those convicts and army officers and men and very few women, just Mother and my sister, a few army wives, and a few of their children who were girls? The mass of men about me did not make me feel any particular attraction to them, except, of course, my affection for Father and my brothers. But at night, alone in my bed, my hands exploring my body as of their own will, I thought I glimmered the truth of these matters and put them aside as not proper for thought or discussion during the clear light of day. But even in daytime, flogging as a punishment for affection seemed wicked, and I could not understand why Father acccepted it—though he did.

The Queen's Birthday fell on Monday the 25th of May, some three months after my arrival on the Island. My reforms, even then, seemed to be going so smoothly that I determined to relax discipline for prisoners and soldiers alike on that day, and to hold a day of celebration of Her Majesty's birthday.

I outlined my plans for the day to Major Simmonds. Open-mouthed astonishment preceded his most vehement opposition. Did I really think 2,000 convicts could be trusted to be at large on the Island? Allowed to wander about at will? Yes, I did, provided they were told in advance of what was expected of them, and told that their future rode upon their response to those expectations.

Simmonds did not conceal his view that this venture bordered on the suicidal, that nothing but turmoil would flow from it. However, under some pressure, he agreed not to reveal his anxiety to others.

I told the convicts I encountered on my wanderings of my plans and sought their collaboration. I knew the word would spread, including the word that the continuance of my more lenient regime turned on their reaction to this day of liberty.

A group of convicts among the old hands volunteered to offer a play which was performed, on the evening of that day, first at the main settlement at Kingston and later at Longridge.

I have kept a copy of the playbill printed by Patrick Burke. All prisoners, except those in punishment status, were free to roam the island, alone or in small groups. The same held true for the soldiers, except those on a very few custodial and guarding duties.

On this general holiday, instead of the portion of salted meat which, with maize and a few potatoes, made up the convict's daily ration, fresh pork would be substituted for the salted meat and, what later came to underpin much of the criticism of my work on Norfolk Island, I arranged for the young queen's health to be toasted in a rum punch I had had prepared for the occasion—and very little rum there was in it.

The day went exceedingly well. It started with a twenty-one gun salute from the vessels in the harbour replied to by cannons on the shore. The gates of the Kingston and Longridge prisons were then unlocked and nearly all the prisoners were given the day to roam the island. I wandered amongst them, from group to group, throughout the day. In the evening we held a dinner alfresco for everyone, which I attended with Mary and the children, as did quite a few of the military officers and their families, after which fireworks were set off for all to enjoy. The plays were performed—*The Castle of Andalusia* and the tent scene from *Richard II*—followed by some short, comic, music-hall turns by several convicts, and a vigorous hornpipe danced by Michael Burns, who had before my arrival suffered over 2,000 lashes for various minor crimes, as well as almost two years in confinement, much of it in solitary, and at least six months on a diet of bread and water. I found it amazing that with such punishment behind him he could find the heart and the strength to entertain us all. Then came the national anthem. The bugle blew and all returned to their quarters.

I had warned the prisoners that on their behavior on this day much depended for their future treatment. Let them prove that they could be trusted with a greater freedom. I was not disappointed. There were no reports of crimes, or fights, or disorder throughout the day, and rarely has the royal toast been drunk with greater fervor or such impromptu and vigorous cheers.

The fence spoilt the view and the two cannon a few yards from the front verandah, trained on the main convict prison, added incongruity to what was otherwise a pleasant pastoral seascape. Within the first few days of our arrival, Father had arranged the removal of the fence and the cannon, and reduced the number of guards on patrol around Government House. Mother, Catherine, and I were not entirely happy about our lesser protection from the convicts, but Father said that, if they were determined to harm us, the fence and the guns would not stop them, and that they were an irritant to men already sufficiently burdened. As such, he thought they lessened rather than increased our safety.

These early weeks saw great changes to Government House—an incongruous name for what was our relatively modest residence. It is a large, spacious, rambling, one-story bungalow set atop a small hill, rather a knoll, overlooking Sandy or Sydney Beach (I was never sure which was the more popular usage), which is by far the best landing on the island. To a degree, the tall pines hid the architectural horror that was the main prison building, and the overall view was exceedingly pleasant, particularly on brisk sunny days, which came with Oceanic regularity.

The house had been as Father reported to us when he had first seen it: clean, sparse, but adequate. We had brought considerable furnishings with us from home that had mostly been in storage in Hobart Town. Mother recruited several wives of soldiers to help her make curtains and drapes. Swiftly what had looked like an unoccupied barracks turned into a reasonably comfortable home. And there was always the piano on which Catherine and I could continue our fledgling efforts.

My four young brothers, though ordered strictly not to associate with the convicts, roamed the island, and, of course, rapidly became indulged friends with soldier and convict alike. But Mother and Father took a stronger position about Catherine and myself. We were not to leave the close environs of Government House and its burgeoning garden except accompanied by an armed guard. Catherine rather liked this arrangement; the guard provided an entourage for her display of female pulchritude, which was her main purpose in life, or so it seemed to me. And, though I at first found my escorts a nuisance, I quickly learned that properly handled they would not incommode me greatly. I was directed not to engage in any discussions with convicts, though they often called out a friendly but cheeky "Mornin' Miss Minnie" to me, to which I usually waved a reply. I was, however allowed to talk with the convict who ran the small library Father had established for soldiers and prisoners alike—Patrick Burke. Father said he could be trusted.

Catherine and I and our escort took to wandering the island most mornings when the weather was clement, which it mostly was. We would take our sketchbooks and do our best to record something of the scenes we saw. Catherine became assiduous about these wanderings when Lieutenant Edward Hill of the

Ninety-sixth Foot Regiment managed frequently to attach himself to us as our escort. Catherine, as always, responded with what I found embarrassing enthusiasm to any eligible male who manifested his attraction to her—as Lieutenant Edward Hill certainly did. I was being converted into a chaperone, and plainly one that stood too close to her duties for the tastes of those I was chaperoning; but since Catherine was Catherine, and aged but sixteen, there seemed no doubt where my duty lay, and to her annoyance I did not let them out of my sight.

My parents soon started giving dinners for the military officers and the few wives who had accompanied their husbands to the Island, and life on what I had seen as my personal penal banishment gradually improved. And I had my duties: I was to be the school's administrator, a sort of headmistress, making sure that everyone was doing their duty during the half-day schooling for my brothers and several of the other children on the island, the teachers being recruited from the army with occasional assistance from carefully selected, better educated convicts. And Father had the occasional letter for me to draft or copy that helped to understand better what he was trying to do. All in all, the early days on Norfolk Island confounded my expectations; I found I was enjoying myself.

With Mother's encouragement I got out my watercolours and set my easel up, one early morning, to try to capture the scene on the jetty stretching out from the beach as a supply ship was unloaded. I first tried a pencil sketch, but made a mess of it—men too large, ship too small, perspective far awry. It was clear I needed help. I struggled on, but the morning was wasted and made me realise how very much alone I was in such matters. Mother and Father were both too busy to help me, Catherine and the boys were also no help at all, and among the military officers none had shown the slightest interest.

Perhaps I should try to develop my competence on the piano—there, at least, there were training manuals so that I would not be left completely to my own devices. And I did try, but again with depressing lack of measureable success, despite the encouragement of my parents, who would have praised me if I had only picked out a nursery song with one finger.

But there was a band on the island, and Father had great faith in the power of music to calm masculine violence. The band instruments he had bought in Sydney were greatly appreciated, so the convict, Burke, assured me. He also said that there were one or two accomplished musicians on the Island who could, if permission were granted, help me with my efforts on the piano.

I spoke to Father about this, but he was reluctant to have any more convicts at Government House than those who had been house servants on our arrival and who had since served us well. I did not then press the point of my need, but I did not let him escape without his understanding how unfair I thought it for him to impede my social development.

This mixture of adoration and resentment had been with me since my earliest memories of my father. Always I wanted to be with him; and then always our time together, no matter how brief, would be shattered by some claim on him, official or familial, that took precedence over my infantile desires. I would plead for him to stay with me, using the same first words I remember saying to him as a childs, "Oh please, Father."

Mostly, however, I also took reflected pride in those official

claims on him which had disturbed my joy in his company—
he was so needed by others, he was so responsive to his duties.
A childish game of hide-and-seek would have to yield to a
message from the Admiralty or the Royal Geographic Society.
Yet I knew that he devoted more attention to me than to my
sister and brothers—he dealt with them collectively, with love,
but collectively, while to me he occasionally devoted unshared
attention. And then he would be called away. And so, I had
recently developed an acerbity, without wishing it, in our discussions of every topic. The burden of resentment in me was
strong. Every topic could be related directly or by innuendo
to his sacrifice, as I saw it, of his family to his beliefs about
convict governance. And I did not eschew commenting, either
directly or ironically, when he was called away when we were
on the island, that he should not allow his family to keep his
soldiers or his convicts waiting. We both found our conversations upsetting, so that they became fewer and fewer.

All this changed on the Queen's birthday. Father was elated
with the success of what everyone else had seen as his wild
scheme. It had certainly been a joyful and pleasant day for all
on the Island. And the band had proved nearly as much a
success as the two theatrical performances the convicts had
presented. In his enthusiasm, Father mentioned to me that the
leader of the band, a convict named David Ankers, was a fine
musician who had taught piano in London and Sydney.

"Why, then, could he not teach me?" I asked.

I had chosen the moment well. Father said he would check
Ankers's record and let me know.

Later in the day I arranged wih my escort to visit the library
to ask Burke about Ankers. Burke said that he had come to
know Ankers reasonably well over the past few weeks, since
he, Burke, stored the band's instruments for them and arranged

the printing of their music. He thought Ankers a responsible man who would be delighted to get back to teaching the piano. I decided not to report that to Father, but to await his decision.

Simmonds, who had firmly opposed my plans for the birthday celebrations, came smiling to me the next day; of a generous spirit, he congratulated me on its success. I asked how many prisoners had not been let out of their cells yesterday. "Only those on punishment status," he replied. "How many?" I pressed. "About six at Longridge, I think, and probably twenty at Kingston" he replied.

I inquired if those were roughly the numbers in solitary confinement on any one day. Again, he was generous in his reply, "Much the same, though the tally has been decreasing since you came to the Island."

It was now clear to me that in Simmonds I had found precisely the adjutant I needed, a skeptical but loyal supporter.

From this last conversation I realised that I had failed so far, in my wandering about the Island, to visit any prisoners in punishment status; I should have gone to them much earlier. So, later in the day, I went to the Kingston prison for that purpose, having checked on the names and records of several in solitary confinement. Overall, the punishments imposed, months in solitary, often also in irons, some in the dark for twenty-four hours a day, and many there after having been flogged, seemed out of proportion to their offenses—insolence, disobedience, failing to salute, fighting, and so on. The gallows awaited the serious offender. Of course, on these matters, almost everybody disagreed with me, even many of the convicts themselves.

Looking through the list of prisoners, I had noted a name that seemed incongruous, Mick Salmon. I doubted "Salmon" as an English surname; it was probably the name chosen by one whose father was called "Solomon." I knew there were fourteen or so Jewish convicts on the Island because I had been planning to build two chapels, one for the Anglicans, one for the Catholics, and had recognised that I ought to do something, perhaps a special room, for the fourteen Jews.

So, I took with me one of the Bibles, with which our little library was plentifully supplied, so that I could offer it to Salmon, who might be grateful for the Old Testament materials if not for the New Testament.

When I reached the punishment block, I asked to be taken to Salmon's cell and to be left there to talk to him. To my astonishment, the guard refused, politely but firmly: "I'm sorry, Sir. I was ordered to let no one into the punishment cells alone, not even a senior officer. It needs a team of us to get any prisoner out; it's dangerous alone."

My immediate inclination was to reprimand the man vigorously for refusing to obey, or rather for threatening to disobey, a lawful order of a superior officer, which is no small offense; but then it came to me what a difficult position I would be placing him in. The ordinary soldier rarely receives an order directly from anyone of my seniority. The immediate command to keep everyone of whatever rank out of the punishment cells may have been given to him by his sergeant, his lieutenant, or possibly his captain—and there seemed sound reason for such an absolute order, so that the soldier would not doubt its wisdom, and would see himself as bound by its force. I calmed my annoyance and did not press the matter. "Very well. Get some help and bring him out to me here."

It took a while, but eventually Salmon appeared, a well-built man, five foot ten or eleven inches tall, darkly unshaven, with a narrow, slightly uneven face, and a thatch of curly hair; his name in no way concealed his Semitic origins. He was shackled, hand and foot, and escorted by three guards, one of whom grasped a chain that led from his wrists, cuffed in front of him, back between his legs to the guard. It did not seem to me an efficient way of controlling a threatening man; if he could get a grip with his thigh muscles on that chain, it might be turned to service as a weapon. Nevertheless, it was certainly humiliating.

I was sitting behind a table. I gestured toward a chair on the other side of the table. The guards stood their ground. I said to Salmon, "May we talk?" He appeared bewildered, but nodded assent, twisting his head back anxiously toward the guards. "Sit," I said, peremptorily. He did. The guards remained standing behind him. I told them they were not needed. They left, though it was clear that they disapproved of the idea of my being alone with the prisoner. They said they would wait outside, in close calling distance. They did not shut the door behind them.

I asked Salmon if he could read and write, which was not a stupid question since three-quarters of my convicts, old and new, lacked those skills. "Well enough," he replied.

"Good, I brought you this in case it might help to pass the time," I said, handing the Bible across the table.

His handcuffs allowed enough separation of the wrists and hands for him to take the Bible in both hands and set it before him on the table. He murmured, "Thank you."

It started as an interrogation, my asking him about the offense on the Island which brought him to this solitary confinement. He had, he said, been in a fight with another prisoner. I asked why they were fighting. He said that he meant no disrespect to me, but that was a private matter. I let it drop, and asked about his life before he was transported to Australia. There was no way for me to check swiftly on what he told me, but the details did match the sketchy story in his records. I do not think he tried to gloss his history very much in his favour; but, of course, there must have been some polishing— we all do it.

Stilted answers to my inquiries gradually grew into thoughtful replies, and finally into an open, though one-sided, conversation between us, since I was not outgoing about my own life.

I flatter myself that I do listen carefully to what people say, and do match my replies to what I see as the inner truth of what they are telling me. Possibly I deceive myself, but within a few weeks of beginning my regular talks with individual convicts I believe that I developed that skill—of course, previously, no one had ever listened closely to them; they may be responding to the unusual experience of someone at least trying to hear them clearly.

As Salmon talked I noticed that, without paying attention to what he was doing, he tipped the new book up on its spine, separated each hard outer-cover carefully back down to the table, and then, taking a few pages, first left then right, he ran his hand down those pages, pressing them gently from the vertical to the horizontal until he had thus unfolded the whole book. I had seen this done by my bookseller in London, but never by anyone else. Gesturing toward the Bible, I asked, "What are you doing?"

His face relaxed for the first time that afternoon, "Not tearing the binding, not breaking its back," he said. "Allowing it to stay open wherever you leave it."

"Where did you learn to do that?"

"My first job, as an occasional boy, on a property in the North of England. They had a good library, which I was allowed to use on my day off each week, provided I was silent and treated the books properly."

Our talk prolonged itself. One of the guards interrupted to say that it was time for them to go off duty. I told him to get someone to take their place, in order to return the prisoner to his cell when I was finished with him. I added that one guard would be more than enough. In the result, a compromise: through the open door I caught sight of two replacing the three.

Later I tried to summarise my conversation with Salmon. He had been born in the East End of London to German Jews who had fled Germany, for what reason he did not know. He did not think it was persecution; he thought it rather that they belonged to a poor branch of a wealthy family and came to England in the hope of escaping condescension and also in hope of earning their own fortune. In any event, this did not work out at all well. Salmon was the youngest of three children, his two sisters being much older than he. His father abandoned his mother, shortly after Salmon's birth, and went to Canada, where he started another family, but also sent odd drips and drabs of money back to Salmon's mother. The mother and sisters struggled by menial work to hold the family together. He had done well at school, and at the age of sixteen had a full scholarship to the university; but a full scholarship does not pay the rent or feed the body; so he left home for the job of an occasional boy, which his schoolmaster had arranged for him.

All this seemed ordinary enough, but certainly not the typical early career of a twice-transported convict. So, I had asked him bluntly, "A Jewish family, a good education, a reasonable first job—how in Heaven's name did you fall into crime?"

He asked why I was surprised that a Jew should turn to crime. "Do you think we're different, more virtuous, more cunning, less human?" I said I did not think any of that, but the fact remained that of my nearly 2,000 prisoners, only he and thirteen others were of Jewish descent. "That can hardly be chance."

"And how many," he asked, "of your prisoners come from secure and privileged families?"

I agreed that there were indeed very few, and together we tentatively settled on the view that the distinctive feature of Jewish life, which insulated its members from crime and drew them back from crime if they lapsed, was the sense of acceptance and protection by a loving family. He had cut himself adrift, and the anxiety to please which had shaped his first sixteen years, the only male in a struggling family and also doing well scholastically, meant that he would likewise be anxious to please any other group in which he might find himself. And what he found in his first job was a group of servants planning a substantial theft from a feckless master—and he was anxious to please them too. He blended all too well into the convict culture on the journey to Australia and then to elements within it in forceful opposition to the military. And so to Norfolk Island.

"But why still in trouble here?"

"The Ring," he said. His reply troubled me. Simmonds had spoken to me about The Ring, and so had several others of the guards, but it remained only a vague idea in my mind. What, after all, could a gang of convicts do, when all the power, all the control, lay with the military?

It struck me that there may be more to Salmon's idea that

the social cohesion of the Jewish family, its willingness to help all within its fold, explained the rarity of the appearance of Jews in prison. Perhaps the persecution that had been inflicted on them, the cruel brutalities of pogroms and the ghetto, had developed that cohesion in a way not known to those who had not had to suffer as a group. And in this sense, prisoners could be seen as banding together against their guards for similar reasons. Perhaps that idea also helped to explain gangs in prisons, in particular The Ring.

I did not pursue the matter with Salmon, but arranged for him to be returned to his cell, having agreed to consider a different job for him when he was released back to the general population of the prison. He had been working as an agricultural hand; that seemed a waste in the light of his education.

I would talk to the prisoner, Patrick Burke, about Salmon. Perhaps Salmon could help in the library.

Soon after the Queen's birthday, Maconochie came to the library to ask what I knew about a prisoner named Salmon and whether I needed help in the library. He suggested that Salmon was at home among books.

I risked no joke about fishy names, confessed my ignorance of Salmon, said that at present I needed no help with the books and the printing press, and asked if I might talk to Salmon and try to find out in what other ways he might be useful.

In agreeing to this, Maconochie gave me his permission to go anywhere on the island, including the punishment cells, so that I could now take something to read to those prisoners in the punishment cells who were sufficiently literate to be interested in reading and were not held either in irons or in the dark cells.

At first, as I wandered the island, I was stopped often. I was careful to halt at the slightest command, and to make appropriate obeisance by touching my cap and bowing my head. The document of permission that the Commandant had given me protected me from other than critical chaffing until, over time, I came to be accepted by the soldiers as part of the scenery of the settlement, but not, I soon understood, by some of the convicts who saw me as "Maconochie's Man," a servile informant who could not be trusted. This was not true, but their perception was just as threatening to my safety as if I had been.

Nevertheless, I did go to the lumber yard to try to find out about Salmon from one or other of the leading members of The Ring. This was not something to be done lightly; I knew the risk, but decided to try to be of use to Maconochie since some of the leaders of The Ring seemed to me to be men of perception who would not assume my role to be traitorous and who might even see that I could be a means of communication of use to them as well as to Maconochie.

As to Salmon, it swiftly became clear that he was indeed in deep trouble with The Ring. They did not take kindly to a prisoner not doing what they wanted of him, and what they wanted was so often contrary to the rules for governing convicts that the lash loomed. On the Island, for the prisoner not in The Ring's good graces, the sea monster Scylla was their capacity to have you injured for not doing what they wanted you to do and the deadly whirlpool Charybdis the prison authorities' propensity to have you flogged for doing what The Ring wanted you to do.

Salmon was distinctly safer in irons in a punishment cell than he would have been in the general population of the island. He had, it seemed, acquired from a complaisant or corrupt guard a substantial amount of tobacco and instead of distributing it, as he should, through the good offices of The Ring, he had tried to cut them out and had sold it himself in small parcels. Further, when they pointed this error out to him, he had refused to give them their appropriate share of the profit. It was, they said, a serious threat to their near monopoly of the island's underground economy and could not be tolerated.

They also made it very clear to me that if it were ever suspected that I had become an informer to the Commandant I would find my situation on a parallel to Salmon's. None of this was conveyed in terms of friendship; they issued edicts reinforced by an ornate scatalogical vocabulary. I paid heed; I did not think they were exaggerating the reach of their authority. I had come to know that the iron fists and sharp knives of the gangs operate in every large prison, whenever any association between prisoners is permitted.

I hoped Maconochie understood this from his experience in Van Diemen's Land, but I doubted he did. Nor could I tell him in the context of The Ring and the Island unless I, too, were to risk their revenge.

I decided to write to Sir George Gibbs about Salmon. Salmon seemed a man who, if Sir George were interested in his case, could safely and promptly be given an opportunity to move to a situation in New South Wales where his criminal past and his convict stigma might not follow him. It was not the sort of letter I wanted to move through official channels, so I wrote it myself soon after I had seen Salmon. Nor did I wish to make Salmon the focal point and only main reason for the letter. And so I couched it in terms of my disappointment in the number of prisoners I had had to punish for their conduct on the Island. I mentioned the increase in the number of crimes against nature that I had had to deal with, but ascribed this to my determination to take this matter seriously, which, I suggested, had not been sufficiently pursued before my arrival. I also mentioned that problems of contraband and of prisoner fighting prisoner were the most frequent offenses, and I added that the latter always seemed to be the offenses of the relatively weak convicts rather than of the strong.

I told Sir George of Major Simmonds' suggestion that there was an explanation for this. Given the presence of theft between prisoners, the strong preying on the weak for anything they might have which the strong desired, the weak had to fight, they had no choice, for if they did not, their situation worsened in the eyes of other convicts and they became even more subject to the will of the strong. They had to put up some resistance, some violent confrontation, if they were not to have an even worse time than we had imposed on all the convicts. And in that resistance, it was not surprising that they usually came off second best in their efforts to fight off their persecutor and that they were the ones more likely to be caught and charged with an offense, for it was one of them and not their opponent who would be found bruised and beaten and lying in the dust. Or it was one of them who had fashioned some sort of a weapon to be the first to strike their earlier oppressor, and were promptly caught. And nor could they inform on their persecutor for that would attract even more convict hostility, and, in the not so long run, might threaten their lives. So it would be off to the punishment cells for the innocent, not the guilty, and there seemed little I could do about it.

The hope of that innocent and punished convict, and it was usually not a vain hope, was that having demonstrated his willingness to do his physical best, poor though it was, to fight off his persecutor, it would become known that to steal from him, or to persecute him in other ways, would not be entirely costless, and he might be left alone.

I added to this the further thought, though I suspect Sir George already knew it, that in a convict settlement like mine, indeed in most every prison, there is a constant search by the guards for anything that can be fashioned into a weapon, for the physically weak had to strengthen themselves sufficiently that they could inflict some harm were they attacked or had they been subjugated by theft or by some other means by another convict whom they knew to be their persecutor.

I told Sir George that I was not looking for sympathy, merely wishing to share with him the difficulty of administering this settlement when first-time convicts were exposed to experienced and relentless prisoners.

Of course, I understood that Sir George could have a sharp and succinct reply to my grousing: was I not the one who had disobeyed orders to keep the old and the new "hands" separate. Nevertheless, I drafted the letter and embedded in it my estimation of Salmon, his background and capacities as I saw them, and my hope that Sir George might see his way clear to make an exception for Salmon and allow his early release to Sydney or somewhere else in New South Wales where he might begin life anew, probably under an assumed name and reinvented history. I did, however, have the sense to decide to return to my draft before sending it as a letter even though a

supply ship was planning to leave for the West the next day.
And looking at the length of my letter—for it had grown with
my uncertainties—I asked Minnie to do a copy of it for me
to work on.

She had several times told me that she enjoyed helping me
in this way, and since we had had our conversation about the
unnatural vice, to which I referred in the draft letter, I did not
think it inappropriate to ask her to copy this one for me,
though it included passing reference to that crime.

Father's letter caused me anxiety. I copied it cleanly for him,
as he had requested, but decided to try to discuss it with him
when he asked for the copy. It revealed what I saw as his
growing anxiety in this whole project; the nearly ultimate pun-
isher who didn't want to punish. And I also thought that it
revealed the essential weakness in his whole Marks System. If
every guard were imbued with his attitude to prisoners, if all
had his understanding and flexibility, if they could all see the
essential humanity behind the violence and misery of the prisoners' lives, and their great difference one from the other, just
as in the world at large, and if they brought to this common-
ality and this divergence Father's humble yet determined desire
to be of understanding and help, then indeed the Marks System would be a superb mechanism of convict governance. But
none of these qualities could reasonably be expected of the
mass of guards, and certainly not of soldiers impressed into
being guards as they were on the Island.

Did this mean that I thought Father's ideas worthless for
running a prison? Not at all. What increasingly seemed clear
to me was that if Father was running a small settlement, say

of a hundred or so prisoners and thirty or so guards, he could sufficiently influence relationships between prisoner and guard, prisoner and prisoner, guard and guard, that a reasonable semblance of his capacity to understand and act accordingly could be projected over the whole group; but if the numbers grew much beyond this, he, or anyone like him, must become a distant and rather fortuitously acting influence, and not much more. He could in a settlement like ours diminish some of its larger brutalities, but its underlying discord and violence would remain beyond his control.

Of course, when I did hand him the letter, and tried to say some of these thoughts to him, they came out scattered and harsh. He listened, and to a degree, responded to my thoughts about the size of a convict settlement, but for the rest he acted as if I was embarrassing him by flattering his personal qualities, which was far from my mind. He did, however, say that he would think again about the wisdom of sending such a letter as this to the Governor—I never discovered whether or not he did send it; certainly he made no further comment about it, nor of any reply from Sir George.

My solitary wanderings kept me in touch, I believe, with the prisoners and soldiers for whose lives I held a degree of responsibility; but they also gave me ample opportunity for anxious reflection on how well or badly my plans were working out. The island gradually appeared more like a settlement than merely a containment for two prisons. However, there was not much change in the working conditions of the prisoners, which remained primitive and harsh, and the lumber yard was still a scene of nearly open hostility between prisoners and guards. Nor had the punishment cells much improved, though the added pains of the lash and of irons had been reduced. I found it hard to know what to do about such matters without losing the support of my civil and military staff.

I came to realise that all the prisons of the world have their own prisons, inner circles of further punishment. The English prisons relied on the convict settlement in Sydney; and that settlement relied on Norfolk Island; and Norfolk Island relied on Kingston prison; and Kingston prison relied on its punishment cells for solitary confinement, with and without irons; and those cells relied on some similarly equipped dark cells, where light does not penetrate; and those cells looked to the ultimate cell, dug deep in the earth and half-full of salt water; and accompanying and behind the whole structure stood the scourger and the hangman. And that is to list only the official, formally imposed, punishments; there was also a host of other informal punishments available at the whim of those who toil in this vast desolation.

Punishment never fails. If the prisoners are well behaved, the value of punishment has been demonstrated; if they misbehave, it is because more severe punishment is manifestly required. And some always behave well, and a few always behave badly, so that the value of punishment is constantly vindicated one way or the other beyond cavil.

I reflected that the spread-eagle, the gag, and the scavenger's daughter were popular subsidiary punishments available to the guards, without control, until I came to the Island. The spread-eagle involved two bolts fixed to the wall of a cell about six feet apart and five feet high, with a third bolt at floor level. The prisoner, facing the wall, was thus fastened and left for whatever period seemed an appropriate sanction for his disobedience or discourtesy. The gag was a short length of round wood with a hole drilled through it; fastened firmly in the mouth by straps around the head, it made a satisfactory whistling sound and tended to ooze blood; a most efficacious technique of silencing the abusive or the loquacious. And the scavenger's daughter taught humility—kneeling, face held down to the knee, trussed like a fowl for the oven.

There is, of course, another less understood consequence of such punishments, less understood but inevitably produced. Many of those who survive them tend to a determined hatred of those who impose them. They band together. They form gangs. They gather power through numbers. Not much worse can happen to them, and in the context of the remote convict settlement, without hope of ever being released, they can become a potent and evil force. Probably, this was the genesis of The Ring.

As soon as I came to understand the extent of random and unauthorised punishments on the Island, I ordered that no punishment whatsoever was to be imposed other than by the Magistrate's Court or after a disciplinary hearing before three military officers, with records of proceedings being kept. Further, as I had previously told the prisoners, I insisted on reviewing, and by no means always approving, every order for the imposition of a flogging. Discipline did not seem to suffer, but it did not break the power of The Ring.

If men are without hope; if their backs are already plowed by the whip and their bodies attuned to frequent suffering, they will band together to kill or injure fellow prisoners who inform on them or seek to oppose them, and collectively they can strike fear into the minds of their guards. I learned these facts from Simmonds and a few of the senior officers and more particularly from Burke, who made clear to me that he was risking his life should it be thought that he was informing on

The Ring. I do not think that by word or deed I broke his confidence.

The Kingston members of The Ring worked mainly in the lumber yard, their power base, from which they controlled the illegal trade in rum and tobacco, and other prohibited goods and services, terrorising other prisoners and corrupting and intimidating many of the guards.

Burke transcribed their oath of brotherhood for me:

> On Earth, in Hell,
> Hand to Hand,
> Sick or Well,
> On Sea or Land,
> On the Square, ever.

> Stiff or in Breath,
> Lag or Free
> On Earth or in Hell,
> You and Me,
> In Life, in Death,
> On the Cross, never.

Almost all members of The Ring had been convicted of a capital crime in Sydney, their execution commuted to life imprisonment on Norfolk Island. They had been bush-rangers, cattle-thieves, pirates, armed robbers; many retained their contacts among criminals in New South Wales and managed to keep in touch with them. I was puzzled how this was achieved, but when I thought of the coming and going of guards, of ships from the mainland, and of mail insufficiently carefully censored the mystery disappeared.

The ineffable fact remains that if you treat men badly enough and you let them live and communicate, they will form potent hostile groups. It is the story of every punitive dictatorship; it is the story of every badly run prison.

Recently, there had been several murders that we could not solve—prisoners stabbed or their throats cut. These were, Salmon suggested, the work of The Ring.

I talked, of course, at length with Major Simmonds about these murders and also with Patrick Burke. Both thought that the killings were the work of The Ring and convict Salmon said he knew this to be at least their claim since he had been quite directly advised by a leader of The Ring he preferred not to name, that he should take particular notice of what happened to those who opposed The Ring's authority. It sounded like the phraseology of a convict with a reputation of leading The Ring, one Westwood known as "Sarge," but I decided not to press Salmon to name him.

It seemed to me that one could not seek to break The Ring until the settlement was otherwise harmonious and reasonably safe and the two prisons less crowded. And, less responsibly, in an anxious and troubled way, I came to appreciate that by now The Ring had become a force for peace and order on the Island, an illegal force but one that as yet I could not conquer without punishing all prisoners on the Island, calling in all ticket-of-leave convicts, putting all in secure cells until the members of The Ring could be ferreted out and . . . what? . . . transported elsewhere or executed, their crimes not having been sufficiently proved. No, I would whittle away at their power if I could, but not confront them head-on—and, in my judgment, this was not cowardly, but prudent.

I spoke to Simmonds about The Ring, avoiding in any way implicating those I now thought of as "my two convicts"—

Burke and Salmon—by mentioning to Simmonds that when I had last visited the lumberyard I had found a distinct smell of tobacco pervading the shed, and yet had not seen any other than convicts there. "Was I mistaken?" He thought not, he said, and confessed to having been long troubled to know what to do about the unruly discipline he found there.

He reported that on one occasion, when some guards had moved to arrest a convict flagrantly smoking a pipe while working in the lumberyard, a group of convicts had surrounded the offender, brandishing shovels, and had threatened the guards if they took any further action in the matter. The guards reported that they had desisted, thinking it best not to provoke what could well have become a riot.

Simmonds stressed that always on the Island his men were vastly outnumbered by the convicts, that immediate physical power always lay with the convicts, except when the soldiers were assembled as soldiers, armed and commanded to fight. When alone, or in small numbers, guards could not have firearms with them—if they did, some would most certainly fall into the hands of the prisoners. Ultimate power may lie with the guards, but even that was doubtful; immediate power always lay with the prisoners. This was one reason, he said, why he disagreed with me in my relaxation of punishments. Severe and disproportionate punishments were all that could keep convicts in check.

Simmonds made a further point that I should have taken into account in my earlier writing on the governance of prisons. There was, he said, often strong distaste among the soldiers for the work they had to do as guards. Major Best had expressed the same point, I realized, in the letter he had left to meet me on my arrival on the Island; but Simmonds took the point further. It was not merely that this was not what soldiers expected to do; beyond that, many if not most of the non-commissioned soldiers had considerable sympathy for the convicts, identified with their hardships, came from the same social backgrounds, even the same communities, had much the same upbringing, perhaps a little better, but not much. They therefore did not see it as a particularly venal sin to form friendships with them, to find gain for themselves by trading with the convicts, indulging their many needs for contraband, not excluding rum and tobacco. It seemed harsh to them, unduly harsh, to flog a man for having a nip of rum or a whiff of smoke.

Put all this together and it was not surprising, he suggested, that groups among the convicts would form gangs to exercise power over other convicts. It was, he said, the way of the world. And he returned to the point that I, as a naval officer, must agree that only by stern and uncompromising discipline, backed up by the lash and the hangman, had the navy managed to maintain its power as a firmly disciplined fighting force.

I disagreed in his conclusion; he went too far there. But the point of the empathy between soldiers and convicts, and, I suppose, between guards and prisoners, gives ample room for the corruption of some of the former by the more manipulative of the latter. A wall of harsh indifference by soldiers or guards, on the other hand, provides ample motivation for the formation of prisoner gangs, by their nature antagonistic to good order and discipline, and with power over other prisoners. A moderate path had to be found.

There was thus a sort of undisclosed but well-understood "contract" between prisoners and those running the prisons. The prisoners would work out their own means of living within the framework of the prison rules, exerting group pressure to maintain order and minimise violence, provided they were not harassed by pettyfogging rules designed merely to manifest the power of the guards and humiliate the prisoners. Failing this, the prison would always be on the brink of riot, and riots would inexorably occur, killing prisoners and a few guards, but also bringing the prison administrators into disgrace with the authorities in Sydney or London or wherever those authorities were. The last thing those authorities wanted was riotous prisons.

I decided I would further my understanding of these matters by a few more visits to the lumber yard. I should not go immediately; I let some time pass after my talk with Salmon, since I knew the fact of that talk would be known throughout the Island, and certainly to The Ring.

He had been among the first convicts I had met on Norfolk Island, and I would not ever forget his mad jerking about when Simmonds and I first confronted him the day I arrived. When I later found out more about him, I could see why he was called "Bony." The skin on his shoulders and back was thick with callouses and scars, in places barely concealing the underlying bones. And, I suppose, the idea of being bone-headed, silly and unpredictable, also had something to do with it. I had been told that though his keepers teased and taunted him, his fellow convicts seemed amusedly protective—and I had witnessed the latter when I first encountered him. On one of my early daily rounds I tried to talk to him, but it was no use—more jerking about and uncomprehending laughter. I checked on his record. It was a brutal and sad story.

He was an orphan, cared for (though I suppose there was not much care in it) in an orphanage until the age of eight, when he ran away, was caught and beaten, so that he ran away again, and this time was not caught. The record is silent until he was fourteen, when he was arrested with others for stealing, flogged, and sent to prison. Again he managed to escape, again was caught, again flogged, and further imprisoned.

When he was released from prison, aged seventeen, he was impressed into the navy—it is not clear whether he had served his full prison term, but that was after all a substantial means of recruitment for His Majesty's ships. He saw action in which he was wounded—a headwound of severity, leaving a lasting scar across his forehead, and, inside his head sudden, fierce rages, particularly when in drink.

Bony was discharged as unfit by the navy. He became involved with other drunken sailors in a fracas with the newly formed London Police in which a policeman was badly injured. He was arrested, tried, and sentenced to death, the sentence being commuted to a further flogging and transportation to Sydney.

In Sydney, he was again in trouble. Again flogged. By now he was seen as totally out of control and a constant danger. He was therefore moved to Goat Island, a small island about fifty feet by thirty feet in the center of the harbor nearly opposite the township. There he was chained to a rock by twenty feet of chain, his shelter from the elements being a box-like construction with holes in the top to admit air, his food pushed ashore in a floating container. His rough clothing became threadbare; his back became a torturous haven for bugs and the brood of the fleas he had brought with him. In occasional agony and unflagging pain, he was totally isolated, except when Sydney sight-seers would throw biscuits and meat to him from passing boats, as one would feed an animal in a zoo.

Someone calculated that he had by this time received over

a thousand cuts of the weighted tongues of the lash—his back, a serried line of scars like the side of an accordion, permanently scarred by the lash and the ensuing maggots that infested the wounds. Before I went to Norfolk Island, Governor Gipps, repulsed by this history, released Bony from Goat Island and sent him on to Norfolk Island to get him out of sight.

Matters did not improve for Bony on Norfolk Island. He was put to work in the lime quarry, carrying bags of lime for transport to the settlement areas. Sweat and the lime became agony for his riven back. Continually in trouble, refusing to humbly obey and by now apparently inured to flogging, he again was disciplined, first by solitary confinement in irons, and then by a further two hundred lashes. It seemed incredible that the debilitated human body could survive such treatment, but Bony did.

And here he had been laughing and jigging about in front of me. His case was not typical; but he represented for me the unthinking brutality of the convict regime. I was at first uncertain what to do about him, but an idea came to me.

Much of the hauling on the island was done by bullocks. Several had become difficult to manage, so that the burden of the work fell on the rest of the herd. I decided to give Bony the care of the recalcitrant bullocks and to let him and them have a shed, well removed from any settlement, in which he could live and from which, I would suggest to him, he should care for the bullocks and try to get them to settle to the plow.

It was a wild idea, but it had no particular risk in it. Bony could threaten no one. The bullocks were not useful at present, and I doubted that he would do them any harm. Maize, potatoes, and some salted meat could be taken to him weekly, and he could care for himself.

After three weeks I rode out to his shack. Bony and two of

the bullocks were at work, a small plot was being plowed, and what looked like a kitchen garden had been started. Bony was no conversationalist, but we managed some communication in which he indicated that he was not displeased with his present situation.

A month later the bullocks, much reformed, were returned to the herd and I told Bony that he could stay at his shack on his now neat little plot of land, growing vegetables in his kitchen garden, until I could find some other suitable work for him.

A week or so thereafter, I remembered that Bony had served in the navy. I asked him if he would like to man the lookout station on Mt. Bates, to keep me informed of approaching or passing vessels. There I built for him another shack, this time of stouter and more commodious construction, topped by a flag-pole from which he could signal the impending arrival of any ship and relay its flag of origin, and any other signals it might be sending. In conformity with this duty and his good naval record, I arranged for the tailor shop to make simple naval working garments for Bony to wear.

Occasionally, particularly when I was depressed with some lack of progress on the Island and felt in need of a longer ride to blow away the cobwebs of self-doubt, I would ride out to Bony's lookout on Mt. Bates. It remained impossible for me to talk with Bony, though it was clear that he understood what I asked of him. He seemed content to sit beside me if I sat, and if I stood he too would stand near my horse so as to pat its neck firmly, but otherwise little passed between us. I knew, without any words, that he was one resounding success of my prison experiment. He would amount to nothing in the view of others, but his pain had ceased, I had lifted the scourge from his back, calmness had come to his mind, and I was confident of his ability to spot, interpret, and report any approaching or visible sail.

The 6th of March, 1841, dawned crisp and clear, with a light summer breeze and a cloudless sky, the island shining as only a small Pacific island can shine. I rose early and determined to give myself a solitary day of reflective stock-taking and celebration. It was, after all, almost precisely a year since I had landed on the Island, and it was also the date in 1788 when the first human settlement was established on this solitary speck in a vast sea.

I walked to rising ground to the north of Government House from where the bulk of my little realm could be observed, its two clusters of buildings at Kingston and Longridge, with their scattering of humpies and houses wandering off to the interior. I had an immodest sense of ownership of my new Eden. Its history was brief; its promise, I told myself, great.

I had hesitated whether this personal celebratory date should be the 10th of October or the 6th of March. Captain James Cook, our greatest navigator, with another great navigator, William Bligh, as his sailing master, had on the 10th of October, 1774, chanced upon this uninhabited isolated island on his journey south from New Caledonia and Melanesia. He had landed and found the island prolific in huge spruce pine trees, with bird life similar to that he had previously seen in his earlier visit to New Zealand, though it appeared that animal life was entirely lacking. He named the island Norfolk Island "in honour of that noble family" and continued his journey to New Zealand. So, probably for the first time in the history of this speck of land, feet had landed on the Island, and minds had judged it suitable for agriculture and human settlement.

Twelve years later, the orders to Captain Arthur Phillip, who commanded the first fleet of convicts to sail to Australia to join the indigenous aboriginals, had included, since there were rumours of French ships in the South Pacific, the following instructions: "Norfolk Island . . . being represented as a spot which may hereafter become useful, you are, as soon as circumstances will admit of it, to send a small establishment thither and to secure the same to us to prevent it being occupied by the subjects of any other European Power."

In my view, March was to be preferred to October for my memorial celebration since I wished to influence life on the Island, not its discovery, and, further, it seemed to me that now was the time to take a risk to achieve better human relationships on the Island.

On the 6th day of March in 1788, the Island was first occupied. On that date, Lieutenant King had landed on the Island accompanied by a complement of seven freemen, nine male convicts, and six female convicts. The free men and the male convicts had been selected as having skills relevant to the establishment of a new agricultural colony. None of the convicts had been convicted of a crime of violence. It seemed an admirable foundation.

The political reality behind this settlement was obvious and in no way concealed. The French had manifested more than a passing interest in the island. Two of their warships, the *Astrolabe* and the *Boussole*, had called at Norfolk Island, but had found the landing too difficult to achieve. Flax and timber had been intended to be collected to be studied in France to determine whether a French settlement should be established. The two ships had gone on to pay a courtesy visit to Botany Bay.

Governor Arthur Phillip decided promptly to preempt these foreign intrusions and appointed Lieutenant Philip King commandant of a new settlement to be established on Norfolk Island. Flax would be cultivated for the sails of the navy; timber cut for the masts of the navy.

The little colony developed well, though the pines proved useless as masts and the flax unsuited to be made into sails. There were only a few records of turmoil or difficulty in the journals of the early years, and they involved the larceny of rum, which was not intended for the convicts, though a tot of rum was within the rations of the freemen and rum was, of course, available to the marines. Otherwise, the early days were marked by the beginnings of a settled agriculture and reasonable harmony between the soldiers, free settlers, and convicts. There is note of several marriages being celebrated, including a marriage between a female convict and a soldier, and another between a male and female convict. Indeed, it was not concealed that Lieutenant King himself took one of the female convicts, Ann Inett, as his mistress, and had two sons by her, naming their first-born "Norfolk."

It did not take long for the home base in Sydney to cure the easy order and growing prosperity of the settlement. Within three months, the first contingent of further convicts arrived. King had selected the freemen and convicts he brought with him with great care; that was far from true of the convicted men and women, and some of their children, who followed.

This first settlement lasted until 1814 when, owing to the difficulty and expense of maintaining supplies, and the considerable expense of a military presence on the Island, settlers and convicts were transported respectively to Port Jackson in New South Wales and Port Arthur in Van Dieman's Land. For a decade, Norfolk Island reverted to its uninhabited, primordial condition.

In 1825 came the second settlement, but this time, unequivocally until my arrival, a place of brutality and severe punishment for the twice transported.

Now, it seemed to me, that in my first year here, there had been a steady movement towards reasonable tranquility and modest productivity. Perhaps I would be able to help to fulfill the dreams of my predecessor, Philip King. We seemed secure and, given our remote circumstances, surprisingly contented. In good humor I decided I should visit the least contented of my flock, those in punishment in Longridge stockade and Kingston prison.

I wandered down the hill toward Longridge, by a path I had rarely, if ever, previously followed. As I came beside a small hut with a smoking chimney, I heard a woman's cry, a high-pitched piercing cry, whether of pain or pleasure I was not sure, but clearly a woman's cry. I rapped on the door with my swagger stick—"Open up."

Silence. I pushed the door open and peered in. A man and a woman hastily covered their nakedness. "Is their trouble here?" I asked, though what was going on was obvious enough. "Come outside," I ordered.

I waited. Reasonably promptly they emerged, clutching their clothes about them, both obviously inebriated, the man more so.

The woman assured me that "There ain't no trouble here, Sir" and the man nodded vigorous assent.

"Your name, my man?"

"Convict Jeremiah Emblin, Sir."

"And yours, madam?"

She made no reply. After a moment or two, Emblin said, "Please, your worship, she be the wife of one of the soldiers. Do he have to know?"

I am not at all sure I did the right thing, but the woman seemed better able to care for herself than did the man, still staggering slightly and of slurred speech. So I told the man to come with me to Kingston stockade, and left the woman to find her own way to whatever was her home—perhaps the hut where I had found them. I made him walk ahead of me. Whether he was drunk or sober, I did not wish to risk a knife in the back.

And so we made our way to Kingston prison where I ordered that he be put in a holding cell and charged with disorderly conduct and possession of prohibited stores, to wit, rum. I then returned to Government House to reflect on the strange turn my celebratory reverie had taken.

The next day I began to investigate what I now thought of as the Emblin Case. I went to my source, not any official source, which would inevitably impinge on my freedom of action, but to my private source, Patrick Burke, whose confidentiality I had come to trust.

He thought he knew of Emblin. "I am told he is a member of The Ring," he said, "I will find out for sure if you want me to."

"And what about the woman," I asked. "Isn't she at some risk from her husband, and perhaps from other soldiers?"

Burke shook his head. "I don't know, Sir, and I can't talk to Emblin about it. It's already known that you visit this library quite often, even when others aren't here. The Ring is already more than suspicious of me. Give me some time. I will try to find out. This place is full of tittle-tattle. Give me some time."

"Of course, but I had better go on to Longridge to see what Emblin has to say."

And so I did. Emblin, sober, was a firmer man than he had

been when I had interrupted his drunken adventure. Yes, he had consumed some rum. Yes, he had been with the woman, but he did not think it the course of wisdom or chivalry, not his words, to tell me who she was. No, he would not tell me who had given him or sold him the rum. Yes, he understood he would be punished, and punished more severely for his contumacious attitude. Yes, he understood a flogging was imminent.

I rather admired him, but hope I did not show it. I would have to wait for Burke's inquiries. In any event I could not hear the charge against Emblin; I was a witness, not a judge, and I would have to be bound by my earlier insistence that such charges should be formally presented and heard, not disposed of summarily.

Later that evening, I discussed the matter with Simmonds. I had discovered that Emblin had not been absent from Longridge without leave. He had permission, when not at work in the lumberyard, to cultivate the small plot of land and build a hut where I had found him *in flagrante* with a woman he said was a soldier's wife. Simmonds' first reaction was the same as mine—a serious disciplinary offense. But why? Were we to be the keepers of morality on the Island, as well as of law and discipline? Adultery, if that is what it was, was a sin in the woman and I suppose in him too, since he knew she was married—or at least he had said so. Were we to punish heterosexual as well as homosexual conduct, the licit as well as the illicit—or, if not licit, at least not criminal? But some allowance had to be made for the rigid, penal settlement, class distinctions between prisoner and guard. The former could not be encouraged to see themselves as equal in status to the latter lest discipline fly away.

Of course, the consumption of rum by a convict was an

offense, but given the affection of the convicts' keepers for rum and its availability to them, some leakage, some pilferage, some sales for goods or services were not entirely unexpected and could hardly be regarded as grave, disciplinary offenses.

Yet, somehow, it seemed a more serious matter than that. Particularly since Burke had suggested that Emblin was prominent in The Ring. In a way his behaviour struck at the very idea of a prison settlement; we were becoming merely an agricultural settlement for temporarily banished criminals and soldiers. Perhaps that is what we should be, but neither London nor Sydney could possibly agree.

My euphoria of the morning had dissipated. My little Eden, indeed! How pretentious. It was inexorably a prison, and must be ruled by a code of law and rules applicable to all on the Island, to all within my jurisdiction. And if soldiers were to be punished for adultery there would be few unpunished, officers and other ranks alike. My idea that the convict could keep the key to his own prison meant that disciplinary rules must be enforced on him until he turns that key completely in the lock of his captivity; so it may well be appropriate to punish Emblin for his adultery or fornication, whichever it was, though not to punish a soldier in a like situation.

I would, of course, avoid testifying at the hearing that I knew that they had been copulating. I would lay more emphasis on the drunkenness. I would not lie; but I would shade my evidence in his favor, and I would respectfully suggest to whoever was hearing the charge that I did not think his conduct merited the lash.

Yet later that evening, I discussed the matter with Mary. She thought I was wrong. Such behavior, she insisted, by the woman as well as the man, should be met with condign, severe punishment.

A chaperone; that's all I have become: a guardian of the chastity and modest behavior of my sixteen-year-old sister Catherine. From our arrival on the Island her interest has been fixed on the younger military officers. Her morning toilet takes an eternity. The care and cleaning of her clothes become a matter of high importance. I am allowed to wander the Island with my sketchbook, accompanied by any soldier who is ordered to watch over me; but Catherine avoids this freedom by regularly making arrangements with one or other of the officers to accompany her on her daily flauntings, and this requires—my parents insist—my accompanying her. She is rather beautiful, I agree, and uncompromisingly flirtatious, so that her being chaperoned is a sound idea; but being her chaperone gives me no pleasure. And her subsequent relentless chatter about the virtues and inadequacies of her latest conquest is hard to endure.

Understandably, I suppose, my Latin lessons had ceased with Father's increased duties on the Island, but so too had my long talks with him about his work and many other matters, and there were fewer letters with which he sought my help. Our family was the backdrop to his work, entertaining the officers and their families at occasional dinners at our fancifully styled "Government House," but otherwise keeping out of the way—proving, I suppose, to anyone who was interested, the distinctiveness and superiority of the upper middle classes.

For my part, I am bored and resentful. This morning I tried to give Father a glimpse of my misery. It was not a very smart idea and it did not succeed. I told him that I had become a nearly full-time chaperone to his other daughter, and I asked if he knew the origin of the word "chaperone." I did not think it French, and if it was French I did not know whence it came. He confessed ignorance of the origin of the word, did not take me up on my scarcely veiled protest about the pattern of my life, and bustled off to the barracks, saying he would ask the chaplain about the word.

Today it was again Lieutenant Edward Hill who was supposed to be taking care of Catherine and myself on our walking expedition. He had been more than attentive to Catherine of recent weeks, and I came to think that my sisterly duties might indeed be necessary.

Their attention to each other began to interest me. She was much less openly flirtatious with him than with others, more attentive to what he said, expressed more interest in his family and in his plans. She even remembered that, unlike most of the other officers, his unit was a detachment of the Ninety-Sixth Regiment of Foot which was now serving in India, so that his was a temporary secondment to Norfolk Island.

For his part, he seemed genuinely infatuated. He was polite to me, of course, but his eyes rarely strayed from my sister to me or to the rest of the Island. His hands too seemed to have a life of their own, resting at every opportunity upon her as she confronted the least hazardous of obstacles.

We walked to a cliff overlooking Slaughter Bay and I tried to settle to a sketch, but I could not concentrate on it. Catherine and Edward sat together a little distance from me, and I had a disturbing sense of their mutual sensuality and of my being a much too proximate chaperone. I felt so much older than Catherine, though only two years separated our ages, but I also felt my anger rising at her and her red-faced beau.

Why should I be angry? Why with him? Catherine was certainly an attractive young woman. I assumed he was single. She was clearly not unattracted to him. Why should he not act as he had? I did not find his conversation, confined as it was to stories about fellow officers and hunting animals in India, at all stimulating, but she seemed to like it. If this was her way of seeking a path away from Norfolk Island, I could understand it: but at sixteen was she in any position to make a sensible judgment about the rest of her life? And, in any event, was that not mainly her business and that of my parents—not mine? I have never disliked Catherine, but I have never warmed to her as a sister should.

I found myself observing their behaviour as if they were animals. When they sat down, they sat so that their hips and thighs were pressed close. His hand would move from a relatively chaste position at her waist, to low on her hips, and so would hers. He would occasionally take her hand in his and rest it in his lap, to what effect I knew not. Glances my way would inhibit their further explorations. And why did I get annoyed? I wonder, did she turn her hand over when he pulled the back of her hand to his lap? Did her hand continue its restless wanderings? Would she know what she was doing? Do I?

In a vague way I understood their lascivious desires, if those were the proper words for them. I had observed and explored, sometimes improperly, my own body, and from my brothers I knew something of the male anatomy, though I could not see how the unmentionable part could hurt anyone, as it was reputed to, unless, like that of male animals in heat, it stiffened to a weapon. Neither my interest nor my annoyance would abate.

Matters moved swiftly with Catherine and Edward. A few days after our walk to the cliff, orders came to the barracks that the segment of the Ninety-Sixth Regiment of Foot, with which Lieutenant Hill served, would rejoin the full regiment in Delhi, traveling by the next available ship to Sydney and then on to India. It meant a long separation for them or immediate marriage, and there was no doubt what the principal actors wanted.

Mother approved, despite Catherine's age, and Father made only formal demures of anxiety rather than opposition. I think I was glad to see her going, with her persistent primping ways, even though I did have some affection for her. Whether Edward Hill would make a tolerable husband escaped me entirely; he seemed ordinary enough and unimaginative enough to be acceptable, and she saw strengths and attractions in him which eluded me.

The wedding itself was a pleasant affair, performed at our "Government House" by the chaplain in the afternoon of the sailing of the ship to carry Lieutenant and Mrs. Hill to Sydney. Catherine was indeed lovely, and Edward, scrubbed and shaved and polished to a high pitch, also looked quite fine.

The band played in our reception rooms, there was dancing, Father broke out the better wines, and generally it was easy to forget for a time where we were and what we were doing there.

I had an opportunity to pay close attention to David Ankers, the leader of the band, whose professional duties as a piano teacher I had solicited, so far without effect. Dressed though he was in convict attire, dark-haired, above middle size, he was as neat and clean in his convict clothes, and held himself as well as any man in the room, not with boastful mien but with quiet authority. In a break in the dancing I asked Father, as a means of renewing my request for piano lessons, if he would ask the band leader to play some piano selections for us.

Father did so, and Ankers played two pieces by Chopin. I was not fitted to judge how well he played, but it was clear he was no amateur. I again pressed my request on Father.

The ship was to sail at high tide at six in the summer evening. We all escorted the bride and groom to dockside, they riding in a carriage, the rest of us walking beside and behind them—it was an attractive scene. Catherine made suitable tearful noises, but I did not think her heart was in the performance; but one can never be sure with Catherine, her emotions are worn so lightly.

Keeping track of the library and the musical scores and instruments kept me reasonably busy, but I have a poor ear for music and little knowledge of musical instruments. At my request, Maconochie gave me permission to receive assistance in that area of my jurisdiction from another convict, David Ankers, who now seemed one of the most highly regarded men on the Island. He had formed and conducted the band for the Queen's birthday celebrations; as a result he was held in high regard not only by the convicts, other than members of The Ring who saw him too as Maconochie's man, but also by the senior army command on the island.

I cannot say that he and I became friends. Friendships are not easy to form in our circumstances. But we did collaborate well in our work and we did talk a great deal about matters other than the staple of convict conversation on the Island—survival.

I had gathered that his conviction in London had been for forgery; he had been sentenced to seven years hard labor and sent to the settlement in Sydney.

I did not press him for the details of these events; but in the course of our conversation he suggested his view of them. In my still brief period as a prisoner, I had learned not to regard what convicts tell me as unvarnished truth—their careers have often shaped their recollection—but I did form the view that Ankers spoke the truth when he said that he was entirely fairly convicted in England. He had, he said, forged another's name on a Treasury Bill. He had done it to help that other, and had gained no personal financial advantage from it. It was, he volunteered, an excessively stupid thing to do. As to the event in Sydney, he was even more reluctant to give details. Apparently, he was having an affair with a recently arrived female convict, who then took the eye of a non-commissioned officer of the New South Wales Corps. The officer claimed some rights in the matter which he, Ankers, had vigorously and excessively resisted. Again, he said, he was stupid to have struck the man. It all had the ring of truth. He was good to work with.

Ankers told me that he had learned from Maconochie that, before he left Sydney, Maconochie had purchased the entire stock of Mr. Ellard's sheet music, as well as a considerable number of musical instruments. There had indeed been some argument with the English authorities as to who would pay for all this—the 43 pounds and 15 shillings. Maconochie thought it entirely appropriate to bring some softening decencies to the lives of those of the convicts who might be at all sympathetic to music. London saw it otherwise, as profligate and wildly unnecessary. In the end, Ankers told me, Governor Gipps had finessed the issue and Maconochie did not have to pay.

The instruments and the sheet music had swiftly proved their worth. There were indeed some convicts, wretched and ill-nourished though they appeared, who retained sufficient energy to have some interest in music. Ankers knew who they were and had formed the band; after a very few practice sessions they had managed an entirely respectable performance at the celebrations of the young queen's birthday.

Gradually the library and its musical adjunct became increasingly popular. Maconochie had arranged a system of "readers" at both prisons, literate prisoners who would read aloud to those of the other prisoners who cared to listen. It was, Ankers and I supposed, his hope in this way to reduce the frequency of homosexual relationships, which seemed to trouble him and the Sydney and London authorities very much more than it had troubled those who ran the Kingston prison before Maconochie's arrival. It seemed to us a hopeless method for that purpose, but a pleasant thing to do for its own sake, and I did my best to find appropriate books.

The convict readers needed books and consulted me often about them, and the convict musicians found sanctuary in talking with Ankers. Gradually, also, a few of the soldiers and officers would drift in to my little office to look for books or, to my satisfaction, to give the library a book or two of their own after they had finished with them. But increased demand soon overtook our meagre supply and I found myself too often importuning the Commandant, when he visited us, for more books.

The trickle of contributions to and purchases for the libary did increase, but remained an inadequate flow. Maconochie did help in one unexpected way. Mail to and from convicts was, of course, heavily censored, so that our news of anything touching our situation was scant, but to my surprise Maconochie arranged for the newspapers and broadsheets from London and Sydney to be put into the library a week after they had come to him or to the military messes. In this way, Ankers and I learned just how tenuous was Maconochie's hold on authority over us.

News of the Queen's Birthday celebrations on the Island had reached both cities. Likewise had reports of the freedoms that Maconochie was allowing the convicts, old and new— tickets-of-leave, their own gardens in what was seen from England as a bucolic, island paradise. Exaggerated stories of the luxury of our lives blended with false tales of the birthday celebrations and found an instant acceptance by the cartoonists and commentators in England and New South Wales. Maconochie was widely mocked as a soft-hearted simpleton with no knowledge of how prisoners must be treated. Was this any way to deter crime at home? Was this any way to treat hardened criminals? None seemed to doubt the answers.

And behind the offensive cartoons and comments lay the grim reality that Maconochie had obviously clearly disobeyed direct orders from Governor Gipps and the English authorities not to change the regime of those convicts who were on Norfolk Island when he arrived—his experiment was to be confined to those of us transported directly to the Island; it was not to be extended to the incorrigible others. Ankers and I feared for his security of tenure, but we feared more for ourselves if the Island were to revert to its pre-1840 regime. Ankers, in particular, would revert to his miserable status as a prisoner, securely held in Kingston prison—not a ticket-of-leave musician, not the bandleader.

We decided we had better become better informed on what precisely Maconochie planned for us. I wound up my courage and asked Maconochie on his next visit if it were possible for the library to include and make available to others the papers on convict discipline he had written and published before he became Commandant. With his approval, I could print and distribute a few copies of these, or of excerpts from them if he preferred. These, I suggested, might help to broaden his already considerable support among convicts and soldiers alike. He assented and Ankers and I began the study of the Marks System as planned by our commandant.

Now that Catherine was gone and I was free of my duties as a chaperone, I decided to try again and with more determination to sketch and paint the scenery of the rugged cliffs of the island and the activities on its shorefront, beaches, and those occupied areas where I was allowed to roam.

When with Catherine, and particularly with Catherine and Edward Hill together, I had sat cheerfully on the cliffside and keeping an eye on them had gone ahead with my rough sketching of a ship unloading at the jetty, or of a column of convicts moving supplies on the beach. Now, with nothing to distract me, I found that I could not with comfort move close to the cliffside. When I did, an urge to throw myself down to the rocks below would come to me—no, that is not right, not so much an urge as a fear that I would suddenly, for no reason, though deliberately, step off the edge of the cliff and fall to my death. In the result, I chose less anxious settings for my easel.

It troubled me to recognise this impulse in myself. I am young, healthy, privileged, this dull period in my life will pass, I do not have a protracted sentence of banishment like so many on the island. Weirdly, I found I almost envied the convicts with real adversities to confront. I confronted only cloying dullness, inactivity less imposed than self-generated, but without the will to do anything about it.

Through my fellow convict, David Ankers, I gained a window to look into the family world of Maconochie.

Early after his coming to the Island, Maconochie had the iron bars removed from the windows of Government House. There was still a sentry in front and back, but the building had a much less threatening appearance. And from his early days on the Island, he moved unescorted by soldiers freely among us. Sometimes, his wife and one or more of his children were with him; but, of course, when he was not with his family they were always accompanied by an officer or a non-commissioned officer when they left the curtilage of Government House.

The family was often to be seen on the lawns around Government House, but the residence itself was off bounds to all convicts. Domestic help to the family was now provided mainly by the military and by wives of the military who wished to work and earn in this way, not by convicts as had been the custom with several of Maconochie's predecessors (though those convicts who had served in Government House before Maconochie's arrival were kept on).

There was an exception to these arrangements: there was a piano at Government House and Maconochie had agreed to his eldest daughter, Mary Ann, receiving piano lessons from the only person on the Island of a competence sufficient for this purpose—David Ankers.

Hence my view of the home life of Maconochie and his

family. At first Ankers would indulge my curiosity, and I suspect the general human fondness for self-aggrandisement, by detailed reports of his observations; but gradually he became more circumspect, particularly concerning Maconochie's wife and daughters.

There were women on Norfolk Island, wives and daughters of some of the military; but Maconochie's two older daughters, Mary Ann and Catherine, were strikingly more attractive— and they knew it. I do not mean that they flaunted themselves; they did not. But Catherine had carried herself with flirting confidence, and Mary Ann was spirited and direct in her conversation, and was therefore attractive to the more discerning officers. Until Edward Hill made off with Catherine, both daughters had been assets to Maconochie and his wife in the frequent dinners and occasional dances they gave at Government House.

Mary Ann was called "Minnie" by her mother and siblings, but her Father preferred the more adult "Mary Ann." Quite frequently she came to my library, escorted sometimes by her Father, but more usually by one of the military officers, to look through the books and sheet music and borrow whatever she wanted. She was of middle height, comely though not beautiful, swift of movement, of a Mediterranean complexion and dark hair. She and I had frequent and light conversations when she visited the library, and any ticket-of-leave convict there at the time would wish her a "Good Day, Miss Minnie," for her fanily's pet name for her had spread throughout the settlement.

Ankers had told me that when Maconochie had arranged for him to give lessons to Mary Ann, he had checked his criminal and disciplinary records, and had discussed Ankers' suitability for the task with him. There was no doubt of

Ankers' knowledge of music and of the piano; he had taught in London and even official records spoke well of his musical abilities. His offenses in London and Sydney presented no likelihood of his being a threat to Maconochie or his family. More than that, in my few contacts with him I had found him direct of manner, open of speech, and neither excessively humble nor unduly independent; I expected Maconochie had formed a similar opinion.

I did not enjoy hearing disciplinary charges against prisoners, but Simmonds agreed with me that it was a good way to keep one's finger on the pulse of the settlement. Generally, the facts were obvious enough and my role, as I saw it, was to listen with care to the guard's description of the convict's delinquency, to listen with similar care to the convict's story, if he offered one, then to convict the convict of the offense charged, or a lesser included charge, unless there was more than his word supporting his story (or unless, as rarely happened, I found some demonstrable and articulable fault in the guard's story), and then to impose punishment, leaning towards leniency rather than severity, and rarely calling on the arm of the scourger.

Nevertheless, cases of word against word, and nothing more, did trouble me. The case against Fitzgerald was such a case. A guard testified that he had searched Fitzgerald's cell in the stockade at Longridge and had found two pints of rum in a jug in a concealed hole under a floorboard in Fitzgerald's cell. Fitzgerald had firmly denied that he knew anything of the rum, the jug, or the hole, but had offered no suggestion of how all three had come to exist in his cell. I had little choice but to find Fitzgerald guilty; but had not imposed a sentence, saying that I would consider the matter and impose punishment on him at the next disciplinary hearing. Fitzgerald had seemed firm and direct. And so, for that matter, had the guard. I thought I would check on Fitzgerald's original offense and his record on the Island before settling his punishment.

I had become something of a laughing stock to many on the island because of my relentless insistence on cleanliness, but I did not waiver in my war on all filth and bugs in my island jurisdiction.

Even my wife, Mary, and my daughter, Minnie, would both tease me in their different ways on my insistence on a spotless, Irish linen handkerchief to accompany my every tour of inspection of my two prisons—a handkerchief that often came back stained and the worse for wear. Mary said it looked affected; Minnie said it was foppish. It was, I assured them, neither of those; it was my instrument of choice to achieve an effective inspection.

From two founders of the Great Southland, two naval captains of distinction, James Cook and Arthur Phillip, I had learned the prime importance of scrubbed quarters, clean bedding, clean clothes, and an adequate diet for the health of the men under my command.

I had long been impressed by the firm and detailed rules that Captain Cook enforced to keep his crew healthy, far healthier than other ships' crews of his day. By providing a diet rich in natural vitamins and including antiscorbutics like sauerkraut, salted cabbage, carrot marmalade, and portable broth (cakes of meat essence that could be boiled with wheat), much of which the men hated, but were made to eat, and by compelling them to wash and change their clothes with what they found to be irritating frequency, and also by frequent scrubbing and airing of bedding and all the living quarters, he had, in effect, banished scurvy and much infectious illness from his several extended voyages.

These were lessons that I, like other naval captains who had studied his journals, had taken to heart, and had sedulously applied. A ship's safety depended, we believed, in large part on the crew's diet and the ship's cleanliness.

Arthur Phillip had carried the theme further. He had insisted that there be a doctor on each ship of the First Fleet that brought the convicts and their gaolers of the army to Botany Bay. As a result, he too had a record of few deaths and infrequent serious illnesses on that difficult, long, and crowded journey—a loss of life far less than was customary among a crew, let alone among a crew and their crowded and resentful passengers. It was not that the doctors on each ship had specifics to cure illness; rather it was that their insistence on some time for everyone above decks, some regular cleaning below decks, and attention to the quality of the diet for all made the difference. They enforced, in effect, the precepts of James Cook on their vessels, leaving the Captain to attend his other many duties.

This too was a lesson I had learned. A convict settlement had the same needs of an adequate diet and imposed cleanliness as a naval vessel. Bedding must be aired and cleaned, clothes washed, fleas and lice destroyed. And all this must be achieved in the face of the ingrained sloth of convicts and soldiers alike. Also, and it is no minor consideration, convicts should be given some hope that an authority to a degree independent of their gaolers can take note of their situation, of their living conditions, of how they are treated—and a doctor, even a naval or army doctor, can often serve that purpose if he is so inclined, and can become an instrument for minimum fairness.

When I arrived on Norfolk Island with my family and the "new hands" I found it a haven for filth and grime. The prison was rat and roach infested, the convicts' clothes were filthy, and their bedding crawled with bugs. There was no doctor at all for the prison. Somehow I must banish the bugs and delegate the supervision of my settlement's health to someone to oversee it for me, as Arthur Phillip had achieved for his ships.

Lacking animals or men to live on, I do not know if there were fleas and lice on Norfolk Island before men arrived: they probably accompanied the first convicts to reach the Island in March of 1788—I do not believe that Captain Cook would allow a bug to accompany him when he had landed in 1774! But whether indigenous or not, fleas and lice had multiplied prodigiously by the time I reached the island.

Aboard ship, by frequent unannounced and meticulous inspections, it is possible to achieve a high level of sanitation; in a scattered convict settlement, with a prison and a stockade, and many subsidiary huts and buildings, the task is much harder; but I knew it to be central to my duties, whatever many of the men who served under me and many of the convicts thought about my habit of carrying out inspections with a clean handkerchief in my hand to rub on suspicious surfaces to test for grime.

In the senior doctor with the New South Wales Corps, Major Waddle, I found an ally in my compulsive war on fleas and lice, bedbugs and roaches, flies and filth. Major Waddle was seen as a something of a fool by the soldiers until they fell ill. He had been wounded in the leg in his youth, was corpulent, bald, and of unduly ruddy countenance; he did indeed walk with a waddle. I found him thoughtful and direct, vigorously sharing my opinion that by an insistence on the strictest sanitary conditions we could not only save lives and minimize illnesses, but also have a sound influence on the morale of both the military corps and the convicts. With the agreement of Major Simmonds, I arranged that Major Waddle's duties be extended to the convicts and should not be confined to the soldiers, though they would have first claim on his services, and that further medical assistance should be provided from Sydney for soldiers and convicts alike.

Major Waddle joined me enthusiastically in my obsession to make our settlement healthy and clean.

One of our earlier actions had been to have carpenters install wooden floors in the cells at the Longridge stockade. It is impossible to avoid dirt in a cell with an earthen floor, and peculiarly difficult in such a cell to keep fleas, lice, and roaches out of the bedding. In terms of cleanliness, wooden floors were essential, but in terms of facilitating the hiding of contraband they were an asset to the prisoner.

Just as I had found it impossible to run two prisoner regimes on the Island, one for the twice transported, one for the once transported, the "old hands" and the "new hands," so I was finding it far from easy to enforce the denial of alcohol and tobacco to the convicts while they were available, and available in substantial quantities, to the soldiers.

I recalled that Captain Cook had allowed his crew each day a pint of wine, or half a pint of brandy, rum, or arrack, to say nothing of the barrels that were illegally broached in the holds. His were healthy but not always sober ships. I feared that the same was increasingly true of my settlement; in their banishment, many soldiers and, I supposed, some convicts sought solace in the demon rum.

The rations for the soldiers in our settlement were substantial and for the officers, of course, alcohol was not rationed. Likewise, for officers and soldiers tobacco was amply available. In this situation the ban on alcohol and tobacco for the convicts was grossly difficult to enforce, and yet it was unthinkable to Whitehall and therefore to my Sydney superiors that it should not be enforced. If transportation for the convict meant a clean, healthy beginning again, denied none of the luxuries that the law-abiding citizen enjoyed, there would be a rush to crime to achieve a new start in life—so it was axiomatically believed. And would marines serve without their rum ration? Hardly.

This situation suited the Lords of The Ring perfectly. It gave them the opportunity for control of what their fellow convicts much desired. The lumberyard was clearly the headquarters of trade in contraband, but many individual convicts also pursued their own competitive efforts in this market, endangering The Ring's near monopoly. That was probably the reason for Salmon's current painful situation. The Ring had put him there; not the island's official disciplinary processes. I wondered if the same thing was happening to Fitzgerald. Was I, myself, becoming a mere tool of The Ring?

Which brought me back to the case of the convict Fitzgerald.

Mick Salmon told me that he knew what had happened. I had arranged for Salmon's release from the punishment cells at Kingston prison on his promise to cease trading in contraband and I had placed him with a small group of prisoners working on the dairy farm where he thought he could keep out of trouble with The Ring, particularly since he had decided, he assured me, to avoid even the slightest contravention of The Ring's near monopoly of illegal trade. His earlier protracted punishment apparently satisfied The Ring's need for a sanction for his failing to recognise their dominance in contraband, since it had been some time since he was released from Kingston and he remained in good health. I made a visit to the farm and found occasion to talk with him.

Salmon told me that The Ring had been desirous of extending their influence to the prisoners at the stockade. The "old hands" at Kingston were predominantly of English origin; the "new hands," who had come with me on the *Nautilus,* were predominantly Irish. Fitzgerald was, Salmon had been told, prominent among a group of prisoners determined to resist this extension of the influence of The Ring. He did not think they were moved by altruism or a dislike of alcohol, tobacco, gambling, or other available vices—they wanted their own center of power.

Salmon thought it quite probable that the guard informing on Fitzgerald had "found" the loose board in the cell floor, and the hole and the jug and the rum, when he loosened the board and put them there. It was not, he said, at all beyond the influence of The Ring to arrange this for an enemy; many guards were in debt to and under the influence of The Ring.

Fitzgerald, as a leader of the Irish group at Longridge, would never have been silly enough to risk hiding rum in his own cell. If rum were to be available to him, it would be held as safe as could be by another for him—a leader is not be risked in this way. It must be a plot by The Ring.

Assuming that what Salmon said was true, and it did fit my observation of the guard and of Fitzgerald, I remained in doubt how to handle the matter. I had no evidence with which to accuse the guard, and I had already convicted Fitzgerald of possession of contraband. Yet it seemed outrageous to impose punishment on one I strongly suspected to be innocent.

I decided that I would go to the officers' mess to see if Simmonds or Waddle were there. I felt the need to talk the matter through with someone whose discretion I could trust. Both were there. I managed to isolate the three of us with three mugs of the mild beer we were now brewing on the Island.

I did not name my informant, but I told the Fitzgerald story as Salmon believed it to be. "Assume that is so. What should I do?"

Simmonds saw no difficulty in the matter. "Impose an appropriate but lenient punishment on Fitzgerald. We'll keep an eye on him afterwards."

Waddle thought that was the appropriate response, but added a medical twist to it. "I assume he will get some time in solitary. I have recently begun visiting all prisoners in punishment status. I think Fitzgerald will have a minor infection when I call on them. Fitzgerald can spend whatever period of solitary confinement you impose on him in the relative comfort of my new little hospital ward at the prison. He need never know why. He may suspect; but he won't know."

I blessed Arthur Phillip for showing me the collateral values of a sensible doctor.

Captain Maconochie had told me that stringed instruments were not among his purchases in Sydney from Mr. Ellers' stock, so that Ankers' band was confined to drums and wind instruments, and several of them were of a homemade variety—sailors' whistles, and flutes whittled from whatever wood was at hand. Military instruments, the trumpet and bugle and flute, the tin whistle and the bassoon, formed the backbone of the band, but there were also reed instruments, the clarinet and the oboe, as well as a wooden xylophone, and two primitive instruments brought from the Australian aboriginals, a bull roarer and a didgeridoo. Ankers and his allegedly incorrigible convict players did wonders with such a motley collection. They practised regularly in the prison yard, after their working hours, when the weather allowed, and gradually enlarged both their repertoire and their competence.

Ankers discussed with me how best he might approach Maconochie to provide some reduction of his players' work in the mills, yards, and fields of the settlement. There was no doubt, he said, of the players' enthusiasm, but after-hours band practice had its difficulties for ill-fed and weary men.

I asked him about his visits to Government House for Mary Ann's piano lessons. Was there an opportunity to raise the matter with Maconochie there? He said not. The lessons were in mid-afternoon when Maconochie was rarely in the family's living quarters. Had he discussed it with Mary Ann? Yes he had, but she had expressed diffidence in talking to her father of matters concerning the prison, since she had been told by him that she should be careful while on the island to avoid the appearance of ever interfering with his duties.

Ankers had, of course, had it in mind, but I suggested that as the band's competence had improved he might with confidence ask Maconochie, when he next saw him, if the band might not arrange to give regular brief concerts, perhaps weekly on Sunday afternoons, in the yard of Kingston prison, to which not only any soldiers who cared to attend could come, but also such convicts as Maconochie thought proper to allow to be there.

Maconochie approved the plan. After a few weeks, a short concert was given. Many attended, not only from within the prison, but a number of ticket-of-leave convicts who came in from their small holdings, a few soldiers, some with their families, and all seven members of the Maconochie family. Most of the audience sat on the ground in front of the makeshift bandstand. Mary Ann sat with her parents and her brothers in the front row of the lines of seats we had managed to borrow for the occasion for use by the soldiers and their families. Like the earlier birthday celebrations, but on a much smaller scale, this event was accompanied by no untoward behavior. I noted that even a few from The Ring were there in benevolent approval.

As a result, more time was allowed for band practice, several members of the band were given Island tickets-of-leave, and in general the band became an integral and regular part of the life of the settlement. Ankers' stock rose.

Again, with my encouragement, Ankers decided to ask Maconochie if he might ask Mary Ann if she were willing to play a solo piece or two at a concert with the band. Maconochie said that he would speak to Mary Ann about it, and this he did, since when next Ankers went to Government House for Mary Ann's lesson she was full of excitement, he said, at the thought of such a performance.

It was about this time that I found myself becoming anxious for Ankers. Was he risking emotional entanglement with the girl? If so, he was, it seemed to me, in real danger. Had he enough sense to keep his proper distance? His record in Sydney, which had brought him here, did not increase my confidence.

Vulgarly, in convict phrases, I asked him if he hoped to seduce the girl. I think "poking" was the word I chose. He did not bridle at the idea, rather turned my question away; he did not particularly desire a flogging, he said, and he suspected that would be the least of his punishments. I agreed, but said that though I found him on the repulsive side, which was not true, perhaps Mary Ann had a different view of him, and that could also bring its problems for him and, for that matter, for all of us.

To this he responded more thoughtfully. It was, he said, obvious that she enjoyed her piano lessons and liked his teasing attendance upon her, but he didn't think it went further than that. No; he was sure it didn't. And the more he hesitantly affirmed their lack of other than a pupil and teacher relationship, the less confident of his judgment I became. Watching her at that first concert, and listening to Ankers' occasional descriptions of their conversations at the lessons, it seemed to me clear that she was attracted to him—and I could understand it; convict or no convict, he was an attractive, presentable man with an amusing turn of phrase.

I detected no reciprocity of feelings in him. Mary Ann was to him, I thought, an amusing and pretty girl for whom he felt friendship and sympathy, but nothing more. It was his job to amuse and entertain her; this was part of his duty, and it was a duty much to be cherished in his present situation. That was all.

"No, Mary Ann, please, more feeling, less noise!" And he was quite right: my mind had drifted from the music, though my eyes and hands continued to follow the score.

These lessons have become for me the center of each day, five days of the week, with the mornings spent, no matter what I was otherwise doing, in rehearsals of what I might say, the late afternoons and evenings in reflections of what he had said, and what I had said, and what he had replied to me, and what he really meant, and so on.

My mind drifted back to the earlier lessons. Stiff, painfully polite lessons they had been, with a corporal or sergeant ordered to stand by as my escort while the lesson continued. Under my protest that with so many people wandering about Government House in the afternoon I did not need a chaperone, my parents had relented, and we had the piano and usually the room to ourselves.

At the beginning, Ankers had arrived with a soldier guard to escort him to and from Government House, but this too ceased after a few weeks, and he would arrive alone at the back door of our home usually carrying some musical score he had himself prepared for me. Each of our lessons lasted over an hour, gradually more, and gradually they became central to my day.

At first he had stood to the right of the piano while I worked away, or I would vacate the stool to him while he would demonstrate a phrase or two, or an exercise; but again that distance too had greatly reduced, and now he and I shared the stool and our hands not infrequently touched over the keys.

The formality of the early lessons wilted under my genuine interest in him and his life before he came to the Island. And though he rarely risked a direct question, it seemed that he was far from disinterested in me. Increasingly, lessons were preceded by and followed by periods of talk that would terminate with his "I had better be getting back to my work."

And, on the theme of work, I remained troubled that though his professional skills were turned to my assistance, he was in no way remunerated for them; he acted as if amused by this, and assured me that he greatly enjoyed being with me five days a week, and that he would prefer Saturdays and Sundays to be stricken from the calendar.

"Mary Ann, really, you must pay more attention to the music. You are improving markedly but, like all of us, you have a long way to go."

My first hint of a growing problem came in a sentence in a letter to my wife and myself from Lady Franklin, to whom Minnie was warmly attached when we were in Van Diemen's Land, and with whom she had remained in regular correspondence: "I gather Mary Ann's piano teacher is a frequent visitor; she seems most impressed by him."

When Ankers had asked to form the band for the birthday celebrations I had checked his criminal record, and his record on the Island, which was entirely clean. The details of his offense in England were not available on the Island, but forgery, knowingly uttering a forged Treasury Bill, is behaviour much frowned upon by the Bank of England and therefore by Her Majesty's judges and it had earned him a sentence of seven years' transportation, but it does not present any threat to a piano student or a convict settlement. Likewise, his Sydney offense, which had brought him to the Island, seemed to have been of a personal nature, jealous rivalry, which again was no threat to us. He spoke well and was obviously well-educated. When I agreed to his forming the band and discussed the records of those he had recruited to it, I found him direct and courteous, with even an occasional turn of wit.

Minnie did seem an assiduous student, her playing had improved markedly, and I rarely saw Ankers. I knew he visited our quarters several times a week, but at times when I was usually on my daily rounds. I had given him very little thought, except as an asset in my work for the convicts. Pressed by Lady Franklin's hint, I took an opportunity to return from my rounds early when I knew a piano lesson had been planned. Even distant observation confirmed the ease and closeness of the relationship between them; but there seemed no more to it than that.

I had not previously taken note of Ankers, except as a bandleader. I saw now that his clothes were clean and his garments as respectable as a convict's drab can be made. He was above middle height, of dark complexion matching Minnie's, with regular features, and a mop of light, brown hair trimmed to the same abundant shape as when he conducted the band. His manner toward Minnie was respectful, but had a teasing and chaffing quality to it which bespoke close mutual understandings.

I spoke to my wife about what Lady Franklin had written and of my observation of Minnie with Ankers. She upbraided me for thinking ill of our daughter. I reassured her that I had no doubt of Minnie's placing a limit on his familiarity, but suggested that my fears were nevertheless great. It would be impossible for her to marry Ankers, and it would be a serious threat to my whole life's endeavor should they form any relationship closer than that of pupil and teacher. The easy relationship between them was already being noted, not the least, I felt sure, by those officers of the Corps who also sought out her company. I was already being unfairly mocked in high places for the Queen's Birthday celebrations and that weak rum punch; if my critics could now add leering innuendos of the debauchment of my eldest daughter by a convict it would spell the certain end of my experiment. The truth did not matter in such affairs; appearance and rumour were everything. My wife rejected my view, but I could see that she too was worried. She said she would speak with Minnie.

Apparently, Minnie did not deny to her mother her affection for David Ankers; she did, however, angrily insist on its propriety and on her right to advance her knowledge and pursue her friendships free from such scurrilous criticism.

Her mother and I talked and talked, and eventually came to a decision. It was quite clear that the piano lessons must cease and that Minnie must see no more of Ankers; I would arrange that—if necessary he could be banished to Bony's hut on Mt. Bates! But the problem of Minnie's future remained. She was now of marriageable age, of good family, with good connections, and reasonably secure financial prospects. She should enter the marriage market. And the Island is no place to do so. She could very likely marry one of the officers, several were in pursuit, but she deserved a better match than that. She could go to my sister in Sussex, who would provide excellently for her until such time as we returned to England. It would be a wrench for all of us—we both deeply loved Minnie, and her brothers would miss her greatly, but it was the right thing to do. Of course, Minnie must be given a choice; if she insisted, she could stay on somewhat longer with us before returning to England, but we would both press on her the advantages of staying with my sister.

Father tried to handle the whole matter by indirection, as if David Ankers had nothing to do with it, which infuriated me. I knew, of course, that with those one loves, and I know he loves me, one is often far from at one's direct best, but Father's circuitous evasions seemed so out of character.

"Minnie," he said, "I think you were right before we came here. We should have let you go home to your Aunt in England. This place is not where you should be."

It was so weakly obvious, so unlike him.

"You suggest I should go now?" I replied.

"Well, yes. Your mother and I have talked about it a great deal and think that that would be a sound course."

Did he really expect me to fall in with this without even mentioning what it was all about—did he think I would be too shy for openness? I had better disabuse him. "And will you then soon arrange the release of David Ankers, so that we can marry when he can join me in England, or better in Sydney?"

"Don't be absurd. You can't marry a convict."

"Why not? When I am of age I certainly can. And you are always telling me the likely worth of all individuals, convicts included, and not to judge them only by their past wrong-doings but rather by their present behavior. Your whole life here is built on that belief. Why do you change?"

He tried to reassure me that Mother and he were thinking only of my own good, of the much better match I would make in England. I felt a chill of rejection. "You did not oppose Catherine's marriage to Edward Hill. She is your younger daughter, younger than me. David can earn a living quite as well as Edward, probably a lot better if we live in Sydney. You told me you thought well of him. It is only because David is a convict, only to protect your precious penal experiment from ignorant criticism, not for me, that you wish to send me away."

He was overcome by anger in a way I had rarely seen in him. "It is no wish, my girl. You are leaving by the next packet.

Make up your mind to that." And to my despair he turned and left the room.

I had promised to go to Mary immediately after my talk with Mary Ann, but I thought it better first to take a walk around the house to try to calm myself. What joy my critics in Sydney and London would make of this. As it was, the relationship between them would be turned to salacious jollity in the messes and clubrooms. His daughter poked by a convict, and willingly I hear! But if they married, the joke would spread and grow. I knew there had been no carnal relationship between Minnie and Ankers; I knew she spoke the truth. But the truth hardly mattered compared with the vulgar assumption. And marriage would go beyond both. It would spell the end of my time on Norfolk Island. The lash, the spread eagle, the gag would come into their own again. So why did I say it was for her good; why try to deceive her and myself? Ankers was, as she had suggested, probably a better man than Hill. But I had wanted so much more for Minnie; she so merited a first-class marriage; not to become merely a butt for scandal.

It was some time before I felt sufficiently calm to return to the house to talk to Mary. She had not waited but had gone to Minnie in my absence. I found Mary in tears bewailing the unfitness of any relationship with Ankers. Minnie was equally upset, it seemed to me, but was angrily rejecting our plans for her and affirming her lasting affection for Ankers, whatever we did.

There was no use making this into a tripartite confrontation.

It was my duty to act the paterfamilias: "Mary Ann. We shall, of course, talk further about all this; but it is settled. You will be returning to England by the next passage that I can arrange. I will direct Ankers not to come to the house again, and that he is not to speak to you if your paths chance to cross before you leave."

Ankers came to the library in a rage: "I have been kicked out as a piano teacher and must no longer speak to Minnie. If I do, I will be dismissed from the band. It's grossly unfair."

I refrained from any "I told you so." It seemed to me important to calm him down if I was to keep him as an assistant in the library, and also for his own sake. Why he should expect fairness in his situation baffled me; but he did. I reminded him of his assurance to me that he was not unduly fond of Mary Ann. Therefore, he must hold on to what he had, which, given his situation as a twice-transported convict, was better than he could have expected. I also suggested that I thought when Maconochie had time to reflect, and when there was no risk of Mary Ann's behavior causing trouble, he would understand the unfairness of his treatment of Ankers and would likely assist him to return to New South Wales as soon as possible—if only to get him out of the way.

And I made a personal appeal to him, and an appeal on behalf of the other convicts on the Island. "I think that you and I, together, can help to make this a better place for all of us. I believe we are beginning to have some influence with Maconochie, but I think you are now endangering all of us. If you continue any relationship, no matter how innocent, with Miss Minnie, he will destroy you and likely take it out on the rest of us too. And he, too, will 'be destroyed. Quit thinking with your penis and realise what a narrow ledge we walk on."

Ankers took it all reasonably well. Whether he agreed sufficiently to see the need to separate himself from Minnie and to simulate a contrite conformity, even if he didn't feel it, was yet to be seen.

Mary and I waited for an opportune time, when we were alone with Minnie to again raise the subject of Ankers. She was in no doubt what we were about. A usually quickly responsive, warm, outgoing girl was now behaving like a reserved and distant young lady. Nevertheless, I knew we had to have this further talk with her, upsetting though it would probably be.

And it was. Mary had occasional bouts of weeping. Minnie remained hard-eyed and brittle, except when trying to comfort her mother. For myself, I seemed to oscillate randomly between annoyed self-righteousness and a maudlin sentimentality, neither emotion doing me any credit whatsoever.

As soon as the subject of Ankers was raised, Minnie upbraided me. I had always held her close in my love and her vehemence pained me. Did I suspect a carnal relationship, she asked? Of course not. Well then, why should she not respect and learn from a convict? I was constantly trusting them, treating them fairly, could she not do likewise? And what if she and David had fallen in love? Was she to be denied happiness for the sake of my profession, because stupid people would think ill of her and David?

I fear I was obdurate and forceful. I stressed her age (she was just nineteen), her minority, and her dependency. I averred that her mother and I would never agree to her marriage to a convict. In that situation it was unfair both to Ankers and herself to let this affair develop.

My basic position was logical and clear, or so it seemed to me. Any friendship between Minnie and Ankers, other than manifesting a respectful student–teacher reciprocity, was unthinkable, and threatened the whole pattern of our family's life. Her confessed affection for Ankers stressed the need, which we should have seen and acted on earlier, for Minnie to spend the next few years in England rather than in this remote island inhabited by few eligible males. She was too handsome and too talented a girl to be thrown away by this isolation.

Minnie's positon was equally clear. She understood that Ankers, as a convict, was currently an impossible husband, but that may not last. He would, after all, in a year or two be a free man in Sydney, and there was no doubt that he had skills that could support them both in that rapidly changing society. She would not agree to cut Ankers if she encountered him on the Island, and it would be unfair for me, she argued strongly, to have him further punished for no fault whatsoever in his behavior. She did not wish to leave her family and go to live with my sister in Sussex. She would, of course, obey her parents, but she thought it both cruel and unfair to make her friendship with a fine man an obstacle to her happiness. I had, she said, taught her to treat others for what they were, not for what the world thought of them; why would I now desert my own precepts?

Mary was for peace at any price. Every alternative seemed unacceptable to her. The thought of Minnie alone on a journey to England and then living in Sussex separated for years from her family caused Mary to weep. Though she well understood

its purpose, my insistence that Ankers should not further associate with Minnie also distressed her. She agreed that a marriage between an officer of the New South Wales Corps sta-
tioned on the Island was a sad match for her to contemplate,
and she agreed that that seemed likely if Minnie were to stay
with us.

In the end I prevailed; authority often does. Minnie would
return on the next convenient passage.

Mary, Minnie, and my conscience together troubled me. It
is hard to be sure of one's own motives; there had been such
a mixture of self-interest and concern for my child in this
decision. Minnie's words had hit home; possibly precept and
action were in discord.

At my request they excused me from dinner. I could not sit
there with this turmoil, this rage, within me; my parents' unfair treatment of me left no room for politeness or even silence
in their presence. Though dinner at the table with my parents
would have been impossible, I found that hunger remained,
sharpened rather than dulled by my mixed anger and confusion. I went to the kitchen where, without asking any questions, the convict cook and his assistant fed me well—Miss
Minnie was not to be further troubled, that was quite clear—
and without a word from me.

Later, I went to my room and tried to read, but could not.
I tried to think clearly, but could not. Once in bed, snippets
of unlikely and unfinished conversations between David and
me, between my parents and me, between David and Father,
spun through my head in futile confusion. Ultimately, though,
it cannot have been later than ten-thirty or eleven, I got up,

put on my dressing gown, and walked out to the verandah, the house now being utterly quiet.

The guard, seated on a stool at the corner of the verandah, waved acknowledgment of my presence, but did not call out. I sat down on the steps near where the cannon used to be mounted and looked down over Kingston prison and Sandy Bay.

A few lanterns in the prison and a few in the huts dotting the hillside cast flickering yellow lights over the moonlit scene.

I wondered whether David was awake and whether he yet knew of my parents' sudden turn against us. I doubted it. Everything had happened so quickly today. Father would not involve David until he had settled my future—that was one of the things I objected to, David being treated as just another convict.

It was so monstrously unfair. Neither of us, David nor I, had done anything, anything at all, to deserve this treatment. I knew I loved David and I felt sure he loved me—though he had never expressly said so, his eyes and gentle hands had given him away. But what could I do? I could not remain on the island against my parents' wishes; yet I must not, I will not, give up David. I will write and plan, plan and write, somehow I will keep in touch with him.

My reverie was disturbed by the front door opening behind me and a "Is that you Mary Ann?" from my Mother. "I went to your room, but you weren't there. Couldn't you sleep?" Mother, as always, pretended that nothing had happened. All was for the best—always, relentlessly—except for a continuing series of petty annoyances of which she steadily complained.

"Of course not, Mother. You and Father are ruining my life. It is so unfair."

Mother made a whimpering noise and said, "But it is for

your best, Mary Ann. He is most unsuitable. You will get over him once you are in London. We are thinking only of what is good for you; you must know that; surely you know we love you."

I didn't doubt the love. but I surely doubted what she had said.

Mother sat down beside me and tried to put an arm about my shoulders, but I edged away. "I think you deceive yourself, Mother. Father is thinking also of his precious Marks System and both of you fear scurrilous scandal no matter how unjust it is. I come well after that."

But Mother would not be daunted. Her certainty of the dominance of her good intentions was inflexible. Her certainty that Father cared more for me than for his work was affirmed with equal vigor, but the more she preached their good intentions, the more firmly fixed was my view that to avoid likely and unfair mockery of my Father's plans, my marriage to a good and loving man was to be blocked at all costs.

Father had preached equality between men—even between privileged men such as himself and convicts—each to be judged on his own capacities and qualities. He had preached equality between men and women, even mature and distinguished men such as himself and women—even young women such as me—each to be judged on their own capacities and qualities. He had taught me well, but at the first crisis in my life, when I needed him to act within those precepts, he had refused to consider David and myself, and had been guided by the prejudices of the world.

Mother, on the other hand, had never really approved of the way Father taught me and purported to treat me as an intellectual equal. She professed family and love as her guiding principles, but, like Father, when those values were now being tested all that seemed to guide her was the opinions of others and the need to protect her husband's career.

Both were clearly willing to sacrifice me. And yet I realized that beneath all this turmoil they really did love me.

And then it came to me with sudden insight. How stupid I had been. The kitchen convicts had been too perceptive, silently they had said it all, they must already know, perhaps have previously correctly surmised, this whole story. Nothing like this remains confidential. The knowing smiles in the Sydney and London clubs would be there whatever we now did. Whether I stayed on the Island or left, whether I ever saw David again or didn't, whether even if he and I later married in Sydney or London, the story of the seduction of the idealist's daughter would be told and retold with increasingly false details. And there was nothing I, or my parents, or anybody else could do about it.

I had come to an understanding of just how cold my world could be and decided that for the time being there was not much I could do about it. But as Mother again tried to put her arm around me, the angry turmoil within me overwhelmed me: "Mother, why do you always side with Father? Isn't my life of some importance to you?"

As usual, her reply evaded the hostility in my questions: "You must know, dear, that your Father and I think only of your best interests."

To my mind, this was simply a lie, a repeated lie which infuriated me. They both cared greatly for his reputation, more it seemed than for me. "How can you say that. You don't know David. You don't seem to care that we love one another." But as I argued with her, I knew that the convict cook and his assistant had taught me the truth of this whole matter and that it was useless to upbraid my still very dear Mother in this way.

As a printer, even though a convict printer, I thought it would be useful if I tried to put together excerpts from Maconochie's writings into something like a statement of his purposes. I could print it for those on the Island who might be interested, for whatever reasons. And there seemed a personal interest in it for me; perhaps if I could know his purposes and methods I could expedite my release from the Island.

Maconochie had begun writing in England on the treatment of prisoners, before he came to Van Diemen's Land. Then, while serving Sir John Franklin in Port Arthur, and observing conditions there, he had continued to produce papers for submission to committees of the House of Commons in Westminster, arguing for a very different convict regime. These had led to his appointment to the Island.

Maconochie took no interest in my printing project other than to insist, entirely correctly, that he should be shown the final proposed product before any of it was printed. And he did not object, indeed seemed to welcome, my talking about his plans when he came to the library.

With a few other convicts, from our different perspectives, perspectives very different from Maconochie's, we had formed opinions about his experiment which were quite critical of what he proposed. Indeed, I have found among prisoners almost as much resistance to the Marks System and Maconochie's belief in the efficacy of moral suasion as exists in society at large.

Punishment for offenses on the Island had certainly changed since Maconochie's arrival. The old hands knew this well, having lived under the previous regime, but I recognised it too in the steady changes to discipline and punishment that

Maconochie had introduced since we both arrived. There were many fewer floggings, fewer solitary confinements, irons and chains were being used less frequently, and the gallows was much less frequented.

The old hands told me that before Maconochie's arrival a word of disrespect to any free person on the Island would earn at least thirty lashes, while for any disobedience or slackness in obeying orders, lashes were awarded in the hundreds. Such a punishment, I well knew, would tear a man's shoulders and back to a bloody pulp. But for threats and violence and brutalities between prisoners, other than for killings, the blind eye of tolerance was customarily turned. Few recognised that such a setting was the perfect soil in which The Ring would grow and flourish, facilitating their increasing exploitation of other prisoners.

Maconochie had changed these priorities; minor disciplinary offenses were dealt with by withdrawal of marks or short periods of solitary confinement; but prisoner on prisoner violence was treated with severe punishment. For threatening or striking a guard, the scourger stood ready, but with nothing like the previous excess, and, of course, the hangman dealt with any killings of a convict or a free man if guilt could be established.

Maconochie's disciplinary punishments were thus more lenient than the island had ever experienced, except for acts of violence and for the offense retaining the name of Sodom.

An opportunity presented itself on one of Maconochie's visits to the library to praise him for his declining use of the lash. I said that what I had observed of flogging was that those who survived it were either broken or embittered, the former to the point of conformity, when their behaviour might be observed, the latter to violence and brutality. But I risked direct criticism, saying that I thought the lash particularly useless for "unnatural vice," for which he was continuing to use it. Did he not remember, I asked, the force of sexual desire in the young male? Could he not envisage the sexual pressures on young men in the conditions on the island? Had his naval career not taught him how hopeless was the lash to stop this crime?

Maconochie did not seem to object to the bluntness of my questions. He said that he had arranged for the "readers" in both prisons in the evenings, and for my role in giving them books to read aloud, in the hope of minimising these pressures. He had also hoped that the increasingly free life of the convicts, with their own plots of land to tend and develop, and their own much greater freedom of open association, would reduce this unnatural behaviour. But, unhappily, according to the reports he received, it had increased rather than decreased since his arrival.

I thought that this apparent increase reflected a change in attention paid to such carnal congress between males, since I had been told that previously it had been largely ignored as a disciplinary matter; but Maconochie said that the authorities in Sydney and London would not accept such an explanation, seeing the offense of the utmost gravity under both his and the preceding disciplinary arrangements, and therefore unlikely to be influenced by changes in reporting behaviour. Their view was that it had never been overlooked, but rather, contained by punishment; he believed to the contrary, and so did I, but they were not likely to be easily persuaded.

I further risked telling him, and it was a risk, that several members of The Ring had sexually exploitive relationships with younger convicts, and that some of these were of long duration. Men of The Ring had been well protected under the previous punitive regime, since they were known to the other convicts, and surely to many guards, as dangerous if they were interfered with or informed on. There had not been much change, I thought, under Maconochie's new regime. And as for other transient relationships, they sprang up, lived for a while and died, just as they did, I had been told, in the navy and army—indeed anywhere where young men are herded together and deprived of female companionship. And, of course, the problem is further complicated by a few being by nature inclined to such behaviour, whatever the surrounding circumstances.

"What, then, would you have me do about it?" Machonochie asked. "Ignore it?"

"May I be blunt about this matter, Sir?"

He nodded assent, though with an eyebrow lifted, suggesting some hesitation on his part. Nevertheless, I plunged on. "You should vigorously pursue any coercive sexual subjugation of younger convicts, particularly of 'new hands' who are not yet attuned to prison ways, while turning a blind eye to consensual relationships—unless their presence is forced upon you. You need not publicise such a policy, just act it out for a brief period, and the lesson will be learned. This will reduce the number of reports and sit well with London and Sydney (provided you don't announce what you are doing), while providing firm reaction to the illicit use of force, which is the real threat to the security of this settlement."

One way or another, I argued, consensual relationships should be discouraged but not punished, while dominance had to be strenuously opposed. It was, I agreed, a hugely difficult task.

Maconochie clearly took the point but suggested that, from his naval experience, the distinction between these two types of relationships was often far from obvious (and this was true of many marriages, in his opinion), and given the law as it was, and the prevailing military views of such conduct, he could hardly make disciplinary practice turn on this distinction. He could, of course, let that distinction be borne in mind in imposing punishment.

I recognized the unshakeableness of his conviction and yielded for fear of antagonizing him. "The truth," I suggested, "is that perception often outweighs reality. The conditions that create both the perception and the reality are imposed on you as much as on us. You must live with society's attitudes, we must live in the reality of the prison."

A convict known as "Sarge" was mentioned to me several times by guards and convicts when talking about The Ring. Both Simmonds and Salmon, when I asked them, told me that Sarge was influential in the lumber yard coterie, quite literally a ringleader.

Simmonds gave me some details of Sarge's background which helped explain his influence. I had been wrong in thinking, on my way to the Island, that all the convicts there were twice convicted, once in their home country and once in the Great Southland. Among those there when I arrived was a considerable sprinkling of convicts whose only offense had been in the colonies; they included members of the New South Wales Corps, and earlier military personnel, who had got into serious disciplinary trouble in their military service—repeated absences without leave, repeatedly drunk on duty, and similar offenses, as well as more serious crimes.

Sergeant Major Westwood was such a one. He was the youngest son of a large and modestly successful family that owned a brickworks in Surrey. Apparently from a desire to make his own way in the world, and from a sense of patriotism, he had joined the army and been posted to the Fourth Regiment, sometimes called the King's Own Regiment, which had become a part of the New South Wales Corps.

From its origins in 1789, each Company of the New South Wales Corps consisted of a captain, a lieutenant, an ensign, three sergeants, three corporals, two drummers, and sixty-seven private men. Three, or sometimes four, companies would be under the command of a major, who would also have as part of his headquarters, an adjutant, a quarter-master, a chaplain, a surgeon, and a surgeon's mate. It became common for the senior sergeant of the companies to be ranked as the sergeant major, which made him the then most senior non-commissioned officer. Westwood had risen quickly to that position.

All who know military life know that the role of sergeant major requires forceful character, organising ability, an attention to detail, and a considerable measure of psychological understanding of both officers and men.

In Sydney, Westwood had found time in his off-duty periods to start a farm, marry, and father two children. Using indentured convict labor, the farm prospered, Westwood being particularly adept at selecting hard-working and reliable convicts to work it, and treating them well. He thus could look with confidence to becoming an influential citizen of this new and now thriving community when his tour of duty with the army would end. Like several other officers and men of the Corps, he found no great difficulty in carrying the twin burdens of his military duties and his obligations as a citizen-farmer. His reputation in both capacities stood high.

Trouble came from an unexpected source, a captain, Captain William Burroughs, recently arrived from England to take command of a Company other than the one in which Westwood served. Simmonds had known this captain and described him to me as "a haughty, rather empty-headed, patrician look-ing fellow, with a fine seat on a horse, but not much else to recommend him."

Conflict between Burroughs and Westwood had started with a minor disagreement. Burroughs had taken it into his head that Westwood had deliberately and in an insolent manner failed to "cap" him when their paths had crossed near the barracks—Westwood walking from his farm to the barracks, Burroughs cantering along in full military regalia on his morn-ing exercise ride.

When the matter was raised with him by his own Company Commander, Westwood had refused to apologise. He said that he was in the garb of a farmer, and at the time he did not think Burroughs had recognized him, and anyhow there were only the two of them in an unpopulated wilderness and no harm had been done. Burroughs pressed a very different view of the matter—it was, he said, deliberate insolence. An officer in uniform, a soldier in mufti, the soldier must raise his cap to the officer who will then acknowledge that courtesy by ges-ture or salute—orders were clear. If, of course, the soldier in mufti was hatless or capless, he must raise his hand to his forelock—orders were clear; deliberate insolence.

The petty conflict was papered over, but Burroughs contin-ued critical attention to Westwood's every action. And now, a few weeks later, the story became one-sided, for there was only one left to tell the tale. But this is what Westwood said had happened.

Again they meet in isolation from observers, Westwood re-turning early to work at the barracks, Burroughs on his morn-ing ride. Westwood throws him a marginally acceptable gesture of salute. Burroughs says: "Stand up straight when you salute me, Westwood." Westwood, pushed by this pettiness and later agreeing that he should not have said it, replies: "Surely, we are alone. What stupidity this is." And walks on, openly contemptuous of Burroughs. Burroughs wheels his horse and strikes Westwood across the face with his swagger cane, which he carried as a whip when riding. Westwood grabs the cane, Burroughs hangs on, Westwood pulls him from his horse. Burroughs falls heavily and shouts at Westwood, "I'll see your backbone for that." In a fury, Westwood falls on him. They struggle. But Burroughs' left leg is caught in the stirrup iron; the horse takes fright and bolts, dragging Burroughs bouncing over stony ground. Finally, the stirrup strap breaks, Westwood carries the unconscious Burroughs to the barracks, but Burroughs is dead on arrival.

Westwood told this story to the court martial, recognising that to tell the truth would risk his execution. He was widely believed; it would have been so easy for him to lie, to attribute the death entirely to Burroughs having fallen off his horse and then being dragged. But Westwood confessed that he had struck Burroughs and had thus probably scared the horse into flight.

Westwood was sentenced to be executed. The Governor, pressed for clemency for Westwood by several senior officers and by many of the enlisted men of his company, and perceptive of Westwood's lack of intent to kill Burroughs (though Westwood had clearly intended to strike and had struck a senior officer, which normally suffices to employ the executioner) commuted the sentence to transportation for fifteen years to Norfolk Island. Nor was a flogging administered before he was transported, which would have been customary for such an offense if an execution was spared. The entire colony had heard tell of the "I'll see your backbone" threat, the threat of a severe flogging, and it was thought best to pass over as quickly as possible the far from regretted death of Captain Burroughs.

Westwood's notoriety, rather his reputation, preceded him to the Island where he became known variously as "Sarge" or as Mr. Westwood, depending on whether the convict or the guard speaking his name saw himself as within Westwood's circle of acquaintances or not. And those speaking respectfully to him also included many of the soldiers, for to many of them his story was well known, several had served under him, and he was seen by them as a benefactor rather than a criminal.

I had seen Westwood at the lumber yard and had spoken to him, but he had remained as inconspicuous as he could. He was as neatly dressed as a convict could be, and he held himself with military erectness. He was of dark complexion, of middle height and nuggety build. He sported a typical military moustache, bushy and pointed. I had spoken to him, I recalled, but I had forgotten what I had said—probably some formal inquiry about his duties. He had replied courteously, as I remembered, but there was a dissonance between the words and his eyes which were cold and, it seemed to me, hostile to the point of insolence. Of course, these memories may well have been coloured by what I had subsequently heard about him.

Westwood was, I was told, the major intellectual force behind The Ring. Apparently he had earned his authority ruthlessly, but had exercised it with subtlety. He had managed entirely to avoid disciplinary actions against himself, using others, it was believed, to do whatever threatening, enforcing, or punishing was necessary. I felt the need to talk to him; but I did not easily see how such a dialogue could be arranged. If I went, as I could, to the lumberyard and accosted him there he would obviously be precluded from an open discussion with me. If I ordered him to be paraded before me, and we then had a lengthy and private talk, that would be seen by the officers I worked with as my knuckling under to the gang. I would have to arrange a meeting in some other way; but I didn't see how.

The answer came to me in a dream; a strange, entirely un-expected dream, far from my customary, half-remembered, dull, monochromatic dreams. This was in exaggerated colours, people moving at an ordinary speed, instead of rushing about in futile pursuit, of what I cannot imagine, in my usual though rarely remembered dreams.

I was confronting Westwood, arguing with him, struggling to persuade him of the virtue of my cause—though I did not know what it was I was arguing about. I think it was my Marks System. We were in what looked like a hospital ward. West-wood was smiling at me in a condescending but friendly way, rather as one would smile at a precocious but naughty child, admiring the child's purpose but confident of the impossibility of its achievement. He did not speak, but wandered about, half-listening to my tirade, smiling occasionally and encour-agingly at me. I became more and more desperate, rather as one feels in a dream, running hard but not progressing.

When I awoke, I knew immediately how I could consult with Westwood. Dr. Waddle could arrange it for me. He would pay particular attention to the health of the convicts working in the lumberyard and would in due course order Westwood to the hospital ward in Kingston prison. There was no rush about this; Waddle would handle it with discretion, I knew. And it would not cause comment among either the convicts or the soldiers unless Westwood wished it to—and the risk of this, I decided, was not great.

Within the week I was able to meet with Westwood in the hospital ward at Kingston. He was, of course, perceptive of my little stratagem for our clandestine meeting, and seemed rather amused by it. I decided to be entirely direct with him.

"They tell me, Westwood, that you are the leader of The Ring."

"They do me too much honour, Captain."

"Well, let me assume you know about that organisation. I would appreciate your telling me about it, its purpose, its methods. It may be that together we can turn it to the betterment of the settlement."

He did not respond immediately. Then, he said: "Surely, Captain, you do not expect me to implicate anyone—to draw down punishment on anyone, myself included."

I tried to reassure him that my purpose was exclusively the improvement of my own knowledge so that I might better carry out my duties on the Island. On the other hand, I also told him that I could in no way collaborate in any illegalities or brutalities, and that he should not tell me about them. I wanted to know, I said, how I should handle the gangs at Kingston and Longridge, their conflicts one with another, and the power they seemed to exercise over many convicts, and even over some of the guards.

He did not respond in kind. He made it very clear that his days of trusting officers in authority over him had ended with his trial and sentence in Sydney. He did not even try to conceal from me that he thought of me as a rather foolishly sentimental and untrustworthy adversary.

He was almost patronising, stressing that he saw convict gangs as an inevitable part of prisons, if prisoners were allowed out of their cells in any association whatsoever. This included any prison in which prisoners were required to work out of their cells, and it certainly included all convict settlements. Why should they not band together against oppression? Why should they not scheme and plan to gain such comforts as contraband and, for some, the fruits of gambling could obtain? Why not reproduce, indeed extend, the faults of the society that had condemned them? Everything obtainable in free society was, he said, obtainable to the convict—tobacco, alcohol, sex, clean clothes, better food, more comfortable living quarters, and the respect of his peers—even in such straitened circumstances as Norfolk Island. Only the punishment cells could temporarily interrupt this reality for any prisoner, and they too strengthened the cohesion of the gangs.

All in all, he said, it was very like the army where an efficient sergeant major could arrange for his men to obtain everything an officer enjoyed. He was, in short, firm in his view that he had a role to play in the settlement, and that it was inevitably in conflict with mine.

He agreed with me that the steady increase of the number of convicts with island tickets-of-leave was greatly minimising the conflict between the convicts and the administration. He welcomed this, but insisted that, while the prisons remained, conflict would be inevitable between his purposes and my purposes.

"Would an island ticket-of-leave for you remove leadership from The Ring?" I asked.

"Perhaps it would reduce such influence as I have," he replied, "but within the day another or others would take my place." Of course, he and I both knew that, given his crime and its notoriety in Sydney, I could not possibly solicit Governor Gipps for a larger freedom for him.

I had another idea in mind to test in the acid of his criticism. Would it be practicable, I asked, for a group of convicts from each of the prisons to be recruited as a "hut buildings unit." Timber would be ordered in defined sizes from the lumber yard to assist each ticket-of-leave convict to build his hut on whatever land was given him. The building unit would be under the control of a guard from the engineers in the army, but would otherwise not be supervised, though they would return to prison each evening. The guard would be, in effect, the foreman; he would not be armed.

Westwood thought only for a moment before he replied, "It can do no harm; might make things better for a few of these poor bastards. But until you can let most of us out, and we are not at the mercy of the army, you will have gangs and contraband and corruption. However, should you form that building unit," and this with a half smile, "you should let me help with the selection of its members."

He was indeed arrogant. It was clear that we would not collaborate on many paths to the reduction of fear and violence on the Island unless I would be willing, which I was not, to bend to his will—or he to mine. And of that there was no sign. But I was glad we had talked. It is important to have some sense of your enemy.

Early after my arrival on Norfolk Island I had begun work on two chapels, one for the Catholic majority of soldiers and convicts, the other for the Protestants in both groups—there were, of course, also a few Jews and I determined that in due course I would find somewhere for them to congregate for their religious services. None objected to these efforts, though there was some resistance by the military to ticket-of-leave convicts being allowed to attend general services. Most Sundays I attended the Protestant chapel with my family and gradually a few ticket-of-leave men brooked the military hostility when they recognised my warm acceptance of their presence. But today's service was not one that a convict would be fool enough to attend.

It was the first funeral service for a soldier killed by a prisoner since my arrival on the island.

One evening, earlier in the week, twelve convicts, all "old hands," were rowed out to the supply ship *Governor Phillip* preparatory to starting unloading her the next day. They had planned to try to take her over and escape, but found not only the crew aboard, as they expected, but also a small detachment of soldiers. Nevertheless, foolhardy, they went ahead with their plans and for a few minutes it appeared that they would succeed. Thereafter the soldiers proved too much for the convicts, four were shot and killed, several wounded, and the rest taken captive. In the melee one soldier was killed.

The funeral service was for the soldier; the dead convicts had already been buried in the convict cemetery; and arrangements were under way to send the surviving attempted escapees back to Sydney for trial.

I had found the service deeply moving; it seemed like a personal failing. The military sentiment was clear; convicts would not try to escape like this if we had been more firm with them—they would have known it was useless. The record of escape attempts were, of course, precisely to the contrary, but I confess even to myself how little I enjoy this sort of criticism to which one cannot with decorum make reply.

After the service I wandered down alone past Government House towards Emily Bay. I found myself meditating less on the escape attempt and the funeral service, and more on the general condition of my island. A few pigs wandered on the open grassland I had to cross to reach Emily Bay.

Clearly, pigs did better on Norfolk Island than people. From records kept by my predecessors, I found that pork had been exported since the early 1800s. And when I arrived there was a thriving trade in salted pork sides, with meat rations carefully protected by the administration since any excess use by the convicts or by the soldiers diminished profits from the export trade.

To preserve the pork for shipment to Sydney and Hobart Town, convict labour had built an ingenious salthouse between Sandy Bay and Emily Bay.

Sandy Bay on the South of the Island is, of course, the site of the Kingston settlement and of the main prison, since it provides a gentle open terrain behind the beach itself, suitable for settlement, whereas the hills rise steeply behind Emily Bay, which lies immediately to the East. Where these two beaches conjoin there is a small promontory. The salthouse sits on that promontory.

Large, shallow rock pools have been chipped out by the convicts at a level where the ocean at high tide and only at high tide flows into them. The sun, plentiful in the South Pacific, heats these pools and daily increases the saline content of the water in them. Then, by convict labour, this highly saline water is carried to large copper vats in the salthouse, with its tall chimney and open smoke louvres. Fires burn under the vats until heavy salt deposits remain for the collection. When I arrived in 1840, it was not unusual for the salthouse to be producing 350 pounds of salt a week.

Whereas pigs and cattle and geese and ducks flourished on Norfolk Island, agriculture remained difficult. The earth covering the hills and valleys of the Island tended to be sparse, in most areas, too light a covering for sustained agriculture. And the pines and maize that had first attracted Captain Cook had proved useless for the naval purposes he had hoped for them.

All in all, my small country was proving a daunting site for a free settlement as well as for a convict settlement. Nature impeded the former, and the paradox of liberty within punishment hindered the other.

Every scrap of further freedom I allowed the convicts had its cost in increased danger to some of them, though increased opportunities for most. Even the first issue of knives to allow them to eat without tearing the meat ration with their hands increased the number of murderous and injurious attacks. It was not that previously they had lacked weapons—any prison which had a lumber yard and any metal work also produces contraband arms—but what they had as weapons were less freely available, less easily to hand, less concealable, and the number of attacks of convict on convict thereby increased in gravity if not in number.

As I wandered my small suzerainty, I had no doubt that all in all the changes I had made were for the better, but their costs weighed on me. The scattered humpies built by the Island ticket-of-leave men, with their few cattle and occasional crops, were vastly to be preferred to the crowded prisons they previously inhabited, and I was convinced these improved conditions had no tendency whatsoever to make men in Ireland or England or Van Diemen's Land or New South Wales more inclined to be transported to them. That was not the cost. The cost lay in the nature and heritage of these men and the women who had accompanied them, both the convicts and the soldiers. Generally speaking, they had been raised in poverty and adversity and hostility by parents (if they had them) who also endured those conditions, and that they had not been weaned from their aggressions by condign punishments for crime was not at all surprising.

I knew my way of treating my subjects was to be preferred to that which preceded me on this island, but I could well see how some men and women of goodwill might disagree.

Soon after Minnie's departure, I resumed my daily rounds. In her last days with us I thought it better to spend more time with my family than usual, since Minnie's situation was a deep sadness, not only to her mother and me, but also to her four brothers.

These walks and rides had no particular pattern. I thought it better to appear unexpectedly wherever I went rather than for my arrival to be expected and possibly prepared for. I did not deceive myself that I was unobserved; I knew as I set out in any direction that my movements were broadly predictable; but I thought it better for all if my inspections and conversations were as informal and unrehearsed as possible.

The shining weather, a sunny day cooled by a light Pacific breeze, lured my steps away from the two prisons and towards some of the huts and small gardens that had been occupied by prisoners who had earned this indulgence. I hailed the back of one man with a "Good morning, my man." He turned and we were both shocked at the sudden confrontation. It was David Ankers, whom I had sedulously avoided since I had arranged for him to be informed by Major Simmonds of the termination of the piano lessons.

I had not planned this meeting, but I determined to make the best of it. He stood silent, the muscles of his jaw firm. He was in no other way overtly hostile. I said, "May we talk?"

"As you will," he replied.

And we did talk, first in brusque and guarded phrases, which slowly softened as we came to communicate on increasingly easy terms. First we stood, a yard or two apart, facing one another, but then at his suggestion, not mine, it should have been mine, we sat side by side on a rough wooden bench outside a vacant hut.

It seemed less, but when I left I found we had talked for an hour and a half, first in a stilted and formal manner, uneasy and hostile, but gradually ameliorating until we were open and direct with one another. Concerning Mary Ann, he understood my point of view though he did not share it; I understood his though I did not share it. Each thought the other wrong, but each did not know what he would have done had our situations been reversed.

It is too painful to recall our talk of Mary Ann, and strangely enough I found that that problem did not occupy most of our discussion. It may well have been the background motif of everything we said; but there was not much to be said directly about it. We understood each other's point of view all too well, and we each felt—I'm sure I did—more than a twinge of guilt, particularly as I came to see something of the qualities in him that Mary Ann had praised. The only note of bitterness in his words to me was his sense of the unfairness in my denying him access to the only piano on the Island. This, he suggested, was an unnecessary cruelty in the light of what I preached about the relationship between behaviour and freedom. He had had the bad luck, he said, to attract the affection of my daughter, through no fault of his own. He had never other than respected and admired my daughter. I should be proud of her; not dismissive. Yes, he did use words like "dismissive." There was no doubt that he was well educated and entirely presentable.

I had, of course, checked what documents we had about him on the island. They were, as usual, sparse. He was the only child of a midlands schoolteacher whose wife had died soon after his birth. His father had not remarried. Both father and son were musically inclined and gave much of their energies to a small local orchestra. They also both taught piano to supplement the family income. Shortly before his conviction he had moved to London, where he was doing reasonably well teaching piano before his London and then Port Jackson convictions brought him to Norfolk Island.

He did not hesitate to let me know that he was well aware of the arrangements that had been made for Minnie to stay with my sister in England pending our return. Why not Sydney, he asked, if it was true that he could earn his ticket-of-leave here and in Sydney before many months would pass. Was she not entitled to make her own decisions when she reached maturity? He was, he said, very fond of her, and given time and a different setting their relationship might well mature into matrimony, provided he could by his own efforts properly support her in Sydney.

I avoided arguing this topic with him, and I did not think he wanted to pursue it. He seemed to be more interested in making clear to me that he understood these matters. And, of course, he also thus advised me that, despite my urging to the contrary, Minnie had in some manner been in touch with him after I had interceded in the affair.

I could, of course, cut off all mail to him, or by him, but that seemed likely only to inflame matters with Mary Ann. And, even then, did I really think it necessary to prohibit correspondence between them? Probably not. So I told Ankers that I would in no way obstruct letters between them or have them censored, as we did with other convict mail. He expressed gratitude, but not with any enthusiasm—as if my decision were obvious.

That was about all that was said directly about Mary Ann, though his access to a piano did keep cropping up and I told him that I would try to make arrangements for a weekly visit by him to my piano when neither I nor any of the family were present. I would have to discuss this with Mrs. Maconochie and would let him know if and when this could be arranged.

Our talk shifted to discussion of conditions on the Island. The change of topic was a relief to us both. He reminded me that he and Burke had been reading my writings on convict discipline, and he expressed a respectful approval of my efforts.

I found myself saying that I would like further to discuss those ideas with him and with Burke, but that now I must return to Government House. I told him I would find an opportunity soon to do so, and left him.

It had been for me a mind-clearing talk. He may or may not be in love with Mary Ann, but he obviously admired her and had grown increasingly fond of her and, as he said, he might well have asked for her hand had their situations been different. I felt relieved that my decision to send MaryAnn back to England was not as unjust as I had feared. I had treated him shabbily, but he had taken it very well. Whether I had been true to my own values was another, very different matter.

Ankers came to the library the morning after his conversation with Maconochie and told me of Maconochie's intention to call on both of us for our reactions to his Marks System. I knew from experience that he would not long delay in doing so. It seemed to me important that we should get our ideas into some order if we were to be of use to him and to ourselves.

Ankers had more prison experience than I; he had been on Norfolk Island for more than a year before I arrived—he had lived under the lash—and his earlier prison experience in England and Sydney had also far exceeded mine. But when you are in prison you give its routines and practises, its opportunities and brutalities and aching dullness, a good deal of thought, and the thought becomes wholly repetitive since little changes. Ankers and I did not differ much in our views.

I tried to take notes of what we agreed on, points that we should try to make to Maconochie if we could. In its essence, we thought the Marks System relied too much on the rationality of prisoners and the reliability of guards.

Maconochie had earlier told the convicts on Norfolk Island that with diligent work and good behavior they could earn up to eleven marks a day, six days a week. With no labor for the government on Sunday and a more relaxed routine, marks were not to be earned on that day; but they still could be lost for misbehaviour, which was never sufficiently precisely defined. Disrespect and disobedience to the guards were grounds for loss of a few marks and, of course, Maconochie could not himself be everywhere, and thus had to rely heavily on the guards' interpretation of what was disrespect and disobedience.

Putting that considerable problem aside, Maconochie had advised us all that a convict of ideal diligence and exemplary behavior could thus earn about 3,000 marks a year, and had further suggested that 6,000 marks would "discharge" a seven-years' sentence, and 7,000 marks a ten-years' sentence. But, when one examined the reality of all this, what "discharge" meant was that Maconochie would then recommend to Governor Gipps in Sydney that a mainland ticket-of-leave should be granted. But the content of the letter of recommendation, the Governor's attitude to our original crime, the needs or problems of the New South Wales community, these were, we thought, the factors that would also weigh heavily with those advising the Governor in Sydney whether the indulgence the Commandant recommended would be granted.

Of course, an "Island ticket-of-leave" was entirely within Maconochie's prerogative and this would certainly follow accumulation of sufficient marks for a "discharge." However, with the settlement of an increasing number of prisoners on their own plots of land, many of whom lacked an Island ticket-of-leave, being allowed to visit or to live in a hut built on that land, the difference that an island ticket-of-leave made to the lives of many convicts was not all that great—merely an opportunity for unfettered movement about the island. It is true that prisoners cherish every element of increased freedom, but paradoxically the increasing liberality on the Island whetted the appetite for a mainland ticket-of-leave.

For the old hands, Ankers insisted, the situation was worse. A New South Wales ticket-of-leave was even less likely to be given by the Sydney authorities. After all, the old hands had already been shipped out from Sydney and Van Diemen's Land as unfit to live there. The case for conditional liberty for them on the mainland was very much harder to make.

It was widely rumoured, and was in fact true, that transportation from England to Australia, other than to Van Diemen's Land and to Norfolk Island, had ceased in 1840, the year that the *Nautilus* brought the first batch of "new hands" to Norfolk Island. Why, then, would it be likely that the New South Wales Governor would welcome this new source of convicts offered by Captain Maconochie? Even if Governor Gipps was interested, as he seemed to be, in Maconochie's experiment, and might be sympathetic to Maconochie's recommendations of our return to New South Wales when a sufficient tally of marks had been achieved, what of his successors?

We were becoming depressed with the thought of unburdening our doubts on Maconochie, but I urged Ankers that we ought to be as clear as we could about it before we talked with him. After all, we were in complete agreement that Maconochie had brought a great healing to the hell that was Norfolk Island before him, that he dealt fairly and openly with the convicts, that he had inhibited the brutality of those of our guards who were brutal, and that he had brought control to the abuse of the lash and the solitary cell. We were grateful to him, very grateful, and we would surely let him know that, but he had asked for criticism, and we should not excessively sugar the pills.

Maconochie might judge how extra marks were awarded for exemplary conduct, but inevitably for the withdrawl of marks for offenses and misbehaviour he was largely at the mercy of and the integrity of the guards and, though he didn't seem to appreciate it sufficiently, also of the power of The Ring. He had to rely on what he was told of indiscipline; in the end, he had to rely more on the word of the guard than the word of the convict. Presumably, he knew this, but perhaps he did not know how helpless we felt under that reality.

And we agreed, Ankers and I, that we would also have to be open about our largest fear: his successor. It seemed likely to both of us, knowing of the newspaper reports of Maconochie's governance of the Island, the cartoons of the Queen's Birthday celebrations, the wildly inaccurate accounts of the bucolic luxury of the convicts' lives, and the lack of cooperation he received from many, both military and civilian, on his staff who would probably be spreading stories of his

sentimental and ineffectual control in Sydney, that Maconochie would not be long on the Island. He had been an unlikely
appointment as Commandant, more senior than most who
were given that job, and widely resented by many who also
had some links to power. If he went, who would succeed him?
And we knew and feared the answer: a disciplinarian with
profoundly different plans for running a prison.

Ankers captured our fears in a phrase: "Maconochie's time
here may also be an island—an island of decency in a sea of
brutality."

I cannot say I enjoyed talking with Burke and Ankers about
the Marks System; I kept wanting to rebut their arguments
and to point out the difficulty of bringing life to my ideas on
Norfolk Island—the two categories of prisoners, the impossibility of rewarding progress with increasing degrees of freedom,
since the prisoner was either on or off the Island, and I could
not control that decision.

Yet there was also truth in many of their criticisms which
were not bound by our present circumstances. To award and
withdraw marks I would have to rely, and so would anyone
else in my situation, on the decisions of others, and those
others may have a very different view from mine of the enforcement of convict discipline. Not only on Norfolk Island,
but in every convict settlement, in every prison, the power of
the guards is considerable, and it could often frustrate policies
and practises imposed from above.

I reluctantly conceded that Marks had failings as a currency
to test for fitness for freedom, while Burke and Ankers agreed
that there seemed no better substitute for a genereal evaluation

of the prisoner's conformity to discipline and personal development than general repute and tested achievement. And there was a further unexpected consequence. Just as marks reported to me and entered into each prisoner's log gave power to the guards, which was difficult to control, so did they give unexpected power to members of The Ring to compel one prisoner to falsely inform about another they wished to control. This brought disciplinary action upon the accused innocent, much as it had on the convict Fitzgerald, against whch it was impossible to defend. We risked becoming part of The Ring's enforcement mechanisms. And it was not easy to obtain untainted corroborative testimony, or to find hard evidence, or to locate guards as witnesses to test the veracity of any story.

I did not find the criticisms of the two convicts compelling except in relation to conditions on the Island, with its two groups of prisoners and the limitations on my authority in relation to a Sydney ticket-of-leave. Absent those two impediments, I still believed that the Marks System held great promise. But I realized that I would have to modify it considerably from its present design; in particular it would require a broader discretion than I was given in relation to Sydney tickets-of-leave, or any equivalent site in which the Marks System might be tested.

Their criticisms could never shake my confidence that in a better prison setting, with guards I had carefully trained, the Marks System would be a vast improvement on current prison regimes. However, given the heritage and realities of the Norfolk Island settlement, I was shaken by the force of their views. And I did not doubt either their gratitude for, or their appreciation of, the many ameliorations of the cruel and stupid regime that obtained prior to my coming to the Island. They were friendly, appreciative, and honest critics, so that their criticisms struck home.

The critique of Burke and Ankers had been chastening for me, but also useful. I had to recognise the peculiar force of their comments about the likely values and means of my successor, whoever he might be.

I found myself pushed back to the comment on my appointment by the Reverend Dr. William Ullathorne, who had visited the Island before I went there. He wrote to me, and the words have stuck in my mind: "On Norfolk Island you will have the worst and most inveterate criminals, the scum of the Penal Settlements to deal with, and hard and unfit instruments in your co-operators. They, and not you, will be in hourly contact with the men and yet what you want is to carry your own spirit with you everywhere. Could you be your own overseers and wardens you might succeed."

I spent a sleepless night after my talk with Ankers and Burke. After nearly four years on the Island, was I merely energetically deceiving myself about my Marks System? And not only deceiving myself, but imposing hardship and futility on my wife and children, even heart-break on my elder daughter, when they and I could well be leading lives of comfort and respectability in England, rather than struggling with hostile prisoners and uncooperative guards in this ultima thule, this distant speck of land in a vast ocean—and achieving nothing!

And yet, it was true that the Island was more peaceful, less swamped in brutality, than it had been when I arrived. Convicts and soldiers now seemed to share some slight sense of building a new land, and not merely existing in and for a prison until they could return to the world. Agriculture was spreading, farms were taking shape, vegetables grew, stock grazed, the feeling of a settlement fell on the Island. Surely the Marks System had played a role in this.

But I had to admit that my reckoning of marks for each convict had lapsed largely into routine. I could not myself keep these books for 2,000 men; I had to rely on others who did not share my enthusiasm for the system, though they fell in with it out of a sense of duty. The peaks and the valleys of unusual good works and serious breaches of discipline found some expression in marks, but the overwhelming pattern was a steady accumulation of a day-by-day allocation, signifying very little about the progress of the prisoner toward fitness for greater freedom.

Perhaps such a development was impossible to measure, but that could hardly be true. Every parent can observe growth toward creativity and conformity or rebellion in a child, why not in a prisoner? Probably that is the point; the parent cares deeply about the child and tries to observe him with under-standing. And it is unreasonable to expect that of a prison guard.

If, then, the Marks System, was not an explanation of the superiority of my regime on Norfolk Island over that which went before—and I had no doubt at all of that superiority—what was the explanation? Merely an insistence on a more humane regime, more fairness, more control of previously un-fettered brutality. But if that is all, would I have been here? Clearly not. Nor would anyone else senior in the administra-tion who was not himself in some serious trouble.

What a ridiculous conclusion: One had to have a bee in one's bonnet about some penal theory before one would will-ingly and humanely fulfill a quite ordinary administrative role.

However, I did not entirely reject the Marks System. Were I running a prison of one or even two hundred convicts, I would be able more reliably to measure the progress of each man towards fitness for a reduction of controls and a larger autonomy—reasonably and accurately measure his stages of growth. And those marks would stimulate and encourage many of the convicts, help them to persuade themselves of their increasing worth. Of course, one difficulty in this, I had to admit, was that quite a large number of convicts were not much interested in changing the pattern of their lives; they liked what they previously had; they simply wanted to expedite their return to that way of life and not to get caught again; and pretending within my Marks System was quite within their willing competence given the attraction of what I had to offer.

It struck me as both sad and funny that my system, fully in place, might be a training ground in dramatic arts, a sort of theatre of acted out mendacity.

What should I expect of my convict charges, not hope for, but expect? Surely not that all would grow towards lawful and contributing lives. Probably only that those who wanted to move in that direction would be helped to do so, and that those who did not would not be made much worse or more dangerous by their prison experience. It seemed a modest enough ambition, but not one that would appeal at all to my superiors in London or Sydney who wanted a regime of harsh discipline to deter future criminality, despite centuries of experience that it did no such thing.

Gradually I gained a wry sense of peace and managed to fall asleep for a few hours before the dawn. After all, I had to admit that I had made neither man nor society and that it would be an achievement if I could help to get rid of practises that made him and them worse. Brutality, aside from the agony caused, clearly coarsened the wielder of the lash and the society that placed it in his hand. To show there was a better way could not reflect badly on my soul. Yet to take a mass of fallen and corrupted criminals and make them better now seemed a romantic and rather silly dream. I could position them all on the path, but each had to choose to step out on it with purpose.

The next morning I decided not to follow my usual rounds of inspection. I needed a quiet time to myself. I would have a long and lazy reflective walk to Mt. Bates to talk with Bony, where we could both sit and contemplate the view in silent accord.

A sentry approached me as I left Government House "Bony reports a sail, Sir."

A supply ship, which had brought a batch of convicts from Sydney, had departed yesterday; no ship was expected for some time. So instead of going there myself, as I had planned, I asked a courier to ride to Mt. Bates, where Bony led his solitary but comfortable life, to see if there was any information about the ship, its tonnage, its signal flags, and so on.

By the time *H.M.S. Hazard* berthed, I knew that the Governor, Sir George Gipps, was aboard. I hurried to welcome him at the dock.

"How good of you to meet me," he said. "I thought I was making an unannounced visit."

I told him how intelligence of his arrival had come to me and said that I hoped he would find occasion to visit the informant, for I was proud of Bony and knew that Gipps would remember the convict he had delivered from Goat Island and would be surprised at his reclamation.

It was good to see Gipps again. I knew that to a degree he sympathised with my ideas on convict discipline and that he had been a bulwark against many unfair criticisms that had beset me in Sydney and London. He told me that he would be on the Island for six days and stressed that he didn't want to put me or my family to any inconvenience. He suggested he might stay at the barracks. I told him that, pursuant to Bony's advising of the imminent presence of the Governor's ship, his quarters had already been prepared at Government House, and that my wife and I would take it as a cruel blow were he not to stay with us.

It began and ended as a most pleasant visit of inspection. Gipps told me that he had been so troubled by the extremely contrary reports he was receiving of life on the Island that he had determined to make this unannounced visit to see for himself.

I told him that I travelled the island alone and unprotected, but I suggested that he should be accompanied by me or by a military officer, and further suggested that he should talk to anyone, convict or free, as he liked, arranging with his companion that he should stand aside, out of earshot, whenever this seemed appropriate. For myself, I would cancel my routine, such as it was, for the next six days so as to be immediately available to move with him, or to be interviewed by him, at his will.

I told him that of the 593 "new hands" who had come with me or been sent to the Island since my arrival, 509 now had Island tickets-of-leave and would be found, after their daily work was done, scattered in huts throughout the Island. I assured him that the remainder were held at Longridge, separated from the "old hands' in Kingston, but I could not conceal the fact that many of the indulgences, including Island tickets-of-leave, available to the former had also been made available to the latter.

Gipps fell in with the arrangements for his inspection of the settlement and travelled widely through the Island, speaking to many prisoners and to those who supervised their work and their living conditions. I went on several excursions with him, showing off, I must confess, my knowledge of many of the men we talked to, their names, their work, something of their background—it is a pardonable conceit, I hope.

Our talks together were harmonious and he was clearly well informed on my failures and my successes. On the evening before his departure, we gave a rather fine dinner at Government House, attended by several senior officers and their wives. The band played. There was dancing. The whole event went smoothly.

At one stage during the evening, Sir George Gipps and I found ourselves in my small library, hiding briefly from the festivities. Each of us had consumed somewhat more than our customary sparse intake of alcohol, and I, for one, felt relaxed and benign, willing to be more open and self-critical than is my wont. Gipps also seemed in a reflective mood. And neither of us was inclined to avoid the subject, out of place though it may be at a dinner and dance, that for the moment most interested us: How should one evalute an experiment like mine on Norfolk Island?

I suppose that it was in my discussion with Gipps that evening that I came to understand the difficulty of persuading the general public, and even my educated peers, of the virtue of my regime over that which had preceded it on Norfolk Island and, for that matter, in New South Wales, Van Diemen's Land, and England. The choice, we tended to agree, lay between a system of revenge, hiding behind the cloak of deterrence, and a system which allowed room for redemption—to my mind a choice between brutality and decency. But Gipps assured me, and I knew, that others thought very differently indeed about the proper result of that choice.

My view was that punishment, allowing room for and facilitating redemption, dignifies society, makes prison service a constructive occupation, and enhances public safety. By contrast, vengeance-based punishment, posing as effective deterrence, demeans society, makes torturers of prison guards, and lessens public safety. Gipps did not disagree with that analysis, but he stressed how few believed in its truth, and how unpopular it was with the politicians and the public we are meant to serve.

I told him that it had been my experience talking with prisoners in England, Van Diemen's, and even more on Norfolk Island, that reliance on deterrence to reduce crime was an illusory goal. No prisoner I had spoken to had expected to be caught, not *this* time; or he had acted in such an emotional firestorm at the time of the crime that nothing else was in his mind, influencing his conduct. Sending deterrent "messages" to potential criminals, based on the severity of the possible punishment tends, I urged, to be a waste of time.

"Are you saying," he countered. "that there should not be a relationship between the gravity of the crime and the severity of the punishment?"

"Not at all. Of course, there should be such a relationship," I immediately yielded, "but though the maximum punitive price of any crime, its maximum punishment, should be declared in advance, the actual, imposed punishment must be adjusted to the varied and often complex circumstances of the criminal event and of the victim and of the criminal." I tried to further develop this theme, suggesting that the criminal law, its police enforcers, its procedures and punishments, did indeed serve as a whole as a deterrent to crime; but that variations in the degrees of severity of imposed punishments had little effect, if any, on all but minor crimes. If this be true, and I urged that all experience suggested it was, then the case for a leading role for facilitating redemption in prisons was strong indeed, as well as according well with our proclaimed Christian ethic.

It was then that Gipps advanced a proposition which I could not easily repudiate. "Believe me," he said, "the proof of this pudding is in the eating. You must show others that your prisoners, when they leave you and return to Sydney or London or Dublin, are involved in less crime than those who leave other prisons in which severe discipline, solitary confinement and the lash spell the conditions of their servitude."

And on this we reached agreement. We will have to trace the life histories of the "new hands" and the "old hands" when they leave the island. But, even then, we both knew, chance would play a huge role in the outcome; the prisoners who came to me direct from Ireland seemed a promising lot who would probably adjust reasonably well to later life, whereas the same may not be true for those who awaited me here in 1840 when I arrived, who may have been too brutalized before my arrival to be susceptible to the beneficent effects of more humane treatment.

All that I could, in all honesty, press upon Governor Gipps was that it was my strong belief that the prisoner grist of my prison mill would do less harm, and possibly more good, to society in Sydney or London or Dublin than those emerging from the hell on earth I found when I reached this island. It seemed to me common sense to so believe. He said that his intuitions agreed with mine, but that they were only intuitions which are often powerless against ingrained emotional prejudices—and that is what I faced.

We both returned to the dance with less spring in our step, though it was now clear to me that in Sir George Gipps I certainly had a sympathetic judge of my work on Norfolk Island.

Before he sailed, Governor Gipps was kind enough to inform me that he would report to England in favourable terms on his visit to the Island. He would, he said, expressly recommend that my extension of some aspects of my Marks System to the old hands should now be approved.

A few weeks later he sent me a copy of his report. It was indeed favourable. He noted the crowded and unseemly conditions still obtaining in the Kingston prison, but made mention of my efforts to improve them. He offered his opinion that my Marks System had had a beneficent effect on both work and discipline and urged that it be further studied with a view to its replication elsewhere. He made no mention of the birthday celebrations nor of the problem that Ankers and Mary Ann had presented. He did report that several of the military officers, though supportive of me personally, thought that my lack of sufficient vigor in ensuring discipline by severe punishment threatened the security of the Island—but he added that he did not share that view.

In his report, Gipps made critical mention of the continuing problem of "unnatural vice" at the Kingston prison, but did not include my explanation of what I had tried to do about it—brighter lighting in the dormitory, arrangements for groups of convicts to be read to in the late evenings, regular monitoring of the dormitories, and vigorous efforts pursuant to any report or indication of an offense to convict and punish the wrongdoer, all of which increased the frequency of reports, if not of the unnatural events.

The report also included mention of dysentery and the sad

fact that, since my arrival on the Island, seventy-five of the new hands had died of dysentery; but he expressly praised my efforts to minimise the spread of disease by improving sanitation and enriching the diet of all on the Island.

All in all, I could not have asked for fairer treatment by a superior officer.

For that reason, the blow fell more heavily. The next dispatch from Governor Gipps was formal and brief. I was to return to Sydney as soon as suitable transport could be arranged for Major Childs, my successor as Commandant. Further orders would in due course be issued concerning my next appointment.

Gipps' report on Norfolk Island had come too late; it had reached London a fortnight after my recall had been ordered. Misreports and rumours had triumphed. Perhaps Burke was right in his criticisms of my efforts, yet his farewell words to me were among the brightest memories I have: "You found Norfolk Island a turbulent, brutal hell; you left it a peaceful, well-ordered community."

Government House.

Overlooking Kingston. Quality Row and officer's quarters in the foreground, with Government House at far right; the prison seen in the distance by the sea.

Part 2

Maconochie and Norfolk Island
after 1844

Of those who figure in this story, only Alexander Maconochie, Mary Maconochie, Mary Ann Maconochie, Catherine Maconochie, Edward Hill, Sir George Gipps, Bony, and Burns were ever in fact on Norfolk Island between 1840 and 1844. The Ring was also there, but its membership is unknown. To my knowledge, there was no convict named Patrick Burke on Norfolk Island, nor a Mick Salmon, nor a David Ankers, nor a Staff Sergeant Westwood. There was, however, a piano teacher whose affair with Mary Ann led to her being sent to England.

Maconochie and his wife and four sons left Norfolk Island in February 1844. They returned to England via Van Diemen's Land (now Tasmania), reaching England in August 1844. For the ensuing five years, with Mary Ann reunited with the family as Maconochie's devoted private secretary, Maconochie wrote about and campaigned for adoption of his principles of prison governance. In October 1849, he was appointed Governor of Birmingham Prison and continued to apply the ideas he had tested in Norfolk Island. Mary Ann never married. She died in May 1855, aged thirty-two.

Maconochie returned to England a disappointed, though not disheartened, man. Despite believing in the success of his penal experiment and despite the expressed approval of it by his immediately senior officer, he had been unfairly discharged, a victim of prejudiced falsehoods spread in England and New South Wales that he had been allowed no chance to controvert.

Prior to 1840 he had used his pen to advance his views on the punishment of crime. He now returned to pamphleteering and energetic personal advocacy, fortified by the loyal support of his wife and the constant help of his devoted new secretary, Mary Ann.

Different aspects of the "Marks System" were advanced in these many writings and speeches, but the essential elements, stated too briefly for complete accuracy, were:

- "Work and behavior" prison sentences instead of "time" sentences
- Marks allotted to measure work and behavior
- Progress or regress in marks being known to the prisoner
- Increasing autonomy within the prison as marks accumulate
- Convict groups to work together with the incentive that each in the group could thus earn more marks than each working separately
- Optional and voluntary cell work available should the convict wish thus to earn extra marks
- Graduated release procedures, including supervision within the community, leading to ultimate freedom

With the years, Maconochie's descriptions of the Marks System changed. At one stage he recommended that the prisoner spend a brief period at the beginning of his sentence in what was, in effect, solitary confinement before he entered upon the marks earning-and-losing stage of his prison term. Thereafter, marks were to be calculated daily and were to be known to the prisoner, as was the total number of marks he needed to accumulate to serve the current stage of his punishment. If approved, he could enter into group work to increase his ac-cumulation of marks, since if each in the group carried their fair stint without adverse marks being awarded they would each earn more than any one of them could on his own— having thus demonstrated an ability to cooperate in labor. Marks could continue to be earned and lost after an Island ticket-of-leave had been earned. The final stage was, of course, sufficient marks accumulated to merit a Sydney ticket-of-leave. As a gloss to these plans: should the prisoner so wish, while he was in prison before his Island ticket-of-leave, he could engage himself in work in his cell that would also earn marks.

The complexity of this system was never realized on Norfolk Island or indeed in Birmingham Gaol. Maconochie's prisoners, new hands and old hands alike on Norfolk Island, had served their earlier term of imprisonment before he became their su-perintendent, and the idea of group collaboration and hence more numerous marks being awarded was never implemented. But, in the main, there was in place a scheme that a given number of marks would reduce the term of years that had been imposed as a sentence. By way of example, earning the maximum number of marks per day would allow the prisoner sentenced to seven years to serve only four years before a Syd-ney ticket-of-leave would be recommended. The quantum of marks was thus used to try to fix the outer limit of the incar-cerative sentence.

But, of course, most of this was theory rather than practice since Maconochie could control rewards *on* the island but not any reward of freedom *from* the island—that was a matter of executive clemency on which he could only offer recommendations—and the prisoners, of course, knew this.

There are, in my view, errors in this "system," both in its general theory and in its particular appplication on Norfolk Island but, before one attacks its details, it is wise to remember that with only these innovative and unpopular ideas to guide him, and despite severe limitations on his freedom to apply them, Maconochie brought a measure of peace to the Norfolk Island convict settlement. A living hell became a conforming prison, relatively safe for prisoners and staff alike. These successes of Maconochie's regime were attested to by contemporary and unbiased observers—his senior officer Sir George Gipps, Governor of New South Wales, and the Reverend Dr. Ullathorne, later Bishop of Birmingham, who had each independently and without interference, leisurely inspected the island and talked to staff and prisoners. And what we know of the later conduct of the convicts released to Sydney and Hobart who had been under Maconochie's charge, "Maconochie's Gentlemen" as they came to be called, suggests that they were disproportionately law-abiding.

One cannot in fairness dispute the remarkable success of Maconochie's regime on Norfolk Island. What one can fairly do is to doubt that its success was attributable to his "Marks System." However, its nucleus—a qualified indeterminacy of punishment, subject to gradual testing of fitness for the next stage of autonomy—has to a degree survived throughout the Western world and has brought some decency and coherence to much of our imprisonment practice. Nevertheless, it is hard to be sure how much his "system" contributed to his success and how much success was attributable to firm, humane, and inspirational leadership.

Maconochie's ideas and his persistent advocacy of them blended not at all well with the official Whitehall position on punishment, which was rooted in deterrence and relied on the infliction of suffering to achieve that end. Contrary ideas like Maconochie's were far from welcome in government circles; but a few men of influence saw their worth and gradually came to his assistance. Of these, the most notable in England was Matthew Davenport Hill, Q.C., the Recorder of Birmingham, who had himself already achieved respect as a penal reformer, being a pioneer in the development of probation. Then in Ireland, Sir Walter Crofton took up the mantle of a disciple of Maconochie and created what became known as "The Irish System" of prison governance, expressly incorporating many of Maconochie's ideas and praising Maconochie for them.

American visitors took an interest in Maconochie's writings and their application by Crofton, with the result that much of the Marks System was embraced as doctrine by American prison innovators such as Dr. Enoch Wines and Zebulon R. Brockway, so that the First Congress of the American Prison Association held in Cincinnati in 1870 adopted a Declaration of Principles (expressly reaffirmed in Kentucky in 1930 at its sixtieth meeting) that incorporated many of Maconochie's ideas and stated them in his words. (See J. V. Barry, Alexander Maconochie of Norfolk Island, Melbourne: Oxford University Press, 1958 at pages 231 ff.)

The English Home and Colonial Offices remained obdurate. The Under-Secretary of the Colonial Office, James Stephen, in a memo that received widespread official acceptance wrote: "Captain Maconochie has not much that is really important to urge.... He propounds the seeming paradox that the object of punishment is not only misstated when it is spoken of as designed to produce a wholesome terror, but that the production of terror in the minds of those who meditate it is to be laid out of account altogether.... I should expect very little real aid in the practical business life from any man who proposes to conduct it by setting at defiance what all other men consider as an elementary truth" (Public Records Office, London, Colonial Office 290/78). Without attributing base motives to James Stephen, such is the power of prejudice and denial among the wilfully ignorant.

It was five years, and under pressure from Matthew Davenport Hill and the Reverend Dr. Ulathorne before the English authorities relented sufficiently in their opposition to Maconochie to allow him a new official appointment, that of Governor of Birmingham Gaol. And even then their determined hostility continued.

What of the island itself after Maconochie's departure? The fears of Ankers and Burke about Maconochie's successor as superintendent of the settlement proved to be well founded. Major Joseph Childs succeeded Maconochie and was indeed a ruthless and perfervid disciplinarian, his administration, according to Sir John Barry, "marked by utter incompetence and debasing cruelties." In July 1846, there was a major riot. (For a biography of Major Joseph Childs, see J. V. Barry, *The Life and Death of John Price,* Melbourne University Press, 1964).

Some details of this riot are worth mentioning, since they illustrate how quickly conditions on the island regressed under Maconochie's successor. The prisoners' cooking utensils at the lumberyard, their "billies" and tin kettles, were confiscated without prior warning, it being the view of the administration that these utensils encouraged the larceny of government supplies since they could be used to cook stolen food. But the prisoners also used those utensils to cook their meager rations, mostly maize, potatoes, and some salted meats. Tempers flared; a riot ensued; five guards were killed and three wounded before a platoon of soldiers arrived to restore order. As punishment, many convicts were flogged and twelve were hanged.

In 1854, the process of closing the entire convict settlement on Norfolk Island began, and was concluded by 1856. Few regretted its passing. Between Maconochie's departure in 1844 and its closing in 1856, the settlement lapsed into a period of extraordinary brutality under Childs and Price, and at the same time became inordinately expensive to manage since it continued to depend for the bulk of its supply on England and the Australian mainland. It was, of course, the cost of supply without recognizable benefits and not the brutality of the regime that spelt its demise.

The island lay uninhabited until 1865 when the numerous progeny of the *Bounty* mutineers were transported by the English government from Pitcairn Island and resettled on Norfolk Island. The families of the mutineers were now seen as heroes rather than the tainted progeny of their allegedly villainous though often envied fathers. They flourished on Norfolk Island and now form the leading citizens of a prosperous community, many bearing surnames of Christian and Whittle and similar appellations inherited from their nineteenth-century English sailing forebears.

It is a beautiful and luxuriant island, with precipitous cliffs rising stark from the sea, a thousand miles from the world. The flora is distinctive, dominated by flax and the tall and shapely Norfolk Pines that first attracted Captain Cook and then the Admiralty to the island, though, being knotted and fragile, they ultimately proved useless as masts for the Navy as had been hoped. The flax was also a disappointment, being unfit for the manufacture of sails. There were no indigenous animals on this island and those that have been imported are treated exceptionally well, being given the right-of-way over motorists, a right they exercise with aristocratic hauteur. Cars halt before leisurely parades of cows, ducks, and geese. For man and beast, life on the island is now unhurried and gentle.

The Superintendent's House (Government House) still stands much as it did when Maconochie's family left it, as do the smaller, but comfortable houses on Quality Row for the senior prison and military officers and their families. The Maconochies and the "quality" overlooked the main prison, where now only its shell remains, and they could also see the gulley leading up to the "new" prison at Lochnow.

Bony's little farm with his originally turbulent bullocks cannot be placed precisely, but one can visit where he lived when he kept his solitary lookout on Mt. Bates, and cured himself from many of his inflicted miseries.

Norfolk Island has become an ideal vacation site for the tourist: low-key, comfortable, excellent food, not overcrowded, enjoying an impeccable year-round oceanic climate, with interesting *son-et-lumiere* depictions of the brutal life of the convict and the Gaugin-like luxuriance of the life of Fletcher Christian and his mutinous colleagues to serve as entertainment, as well as the usual tourist attractions of golf and tennis—though as yet mercifully there is no casino. The hotels are of the three- rather than the five-star variety, but they are comfortable and shiny clean. For those who prefer extravagant fantasy, there is one lavish hideaway accessible only by boat or helicopter.

The life of the island from 1840 to 1844, of most penological interest, is completely neglected, with Maconochie being car-

icatured in the tourist literature as a bleeding-heart sentimentalist who let the convicts get out of control.

Nevertheless, much remains broadly as it was, and it is easy
when on the island to envision the pattern of life there when
the great experiment was under way.

Part 3

WHY DO PRISON CONDITIONS MATTER?

M aconochie's career provokes the question: Why would anyone devote himself to penal reform? If there is a viable alternative, why choose to suffer the chill breath of adverse public opinion, the bemused stares of neighbors, the frustrations and lack of reward? It is a vexing question; a satisfying answer is not easily come by. Yet, down through the history of prisons, penal reformers are legion.

In 1773, John Howard, a wealthy English nonconformist landowner had begun inspections and precise critical narrative descriptions of prisons in Europe and England, and ultimately died in Russia diligently pursuing the same enterprise, far removed from his available, comfortable, and widely respected life in Bedfordshire. *The State of the Prisons* and other writings include much about himself, but nothing directly on the motive for his protracted, self-imposed prison saga.

In 1840, as we have seen, Captain Alexander Maconochie, having succeeded admirably in two careers, drags his wife, his children, and himself to the task of running a convict settlement 12,000 miles from his comfortable home, serves there admirably for four years, is then dismissed and treated as an inept fool by most of his peers.

In 1890, one of the world's leading literary figures, Anton Chekhov, in his early thirties, set out on a 7,000-mile journey, mostly through desolate frozen wastelands over rutted, hardly traceable roads, to the Island of Sakhalin, east of Siberia and north of Japan, the most remote, isolated, and brutal prison colony of the Tzar's penal empire. Six months of his waning and increasingly tubercular life was then devoted to describing a region and a group of convicts far removed from his privileged circumstances in Moscow and the widespread praise of the European literati who courted him. The resulting notebooks consciously excluded literary graces and described the details of convict life in this remote hell of a penal settlement with a contrived detachment barely cloaking his reformist zeal.

In an incomparably lesser way, I have devoted the last five-and-a-half decades to the minutiae of prison regimes in four continents. Yet, a vocation in the academic side of criminal law provided all I needed by way of a comfortable, professional, and personal life. To add myself to the list of prison reformers is not to draw a self-serving comparison. Rather, it is to seek an answer to the troublesome question: *Why should anyone of reasonable ability see the conditions of prison life as meriting serious and sustained concern?*

That human rights are absolute and pertain to all persons, prisoners included, is clearly inadequate. It merely restates the problem. Why should prisoners be included? Many thoughtful persons have been and are prepared to exclude them, write them off.

To suggest, as I often have, that prison is a microcosm of the "outside" world, and thus provides a convenient microscope to observe the human condition, is a true but inadequate answer. It justifies interest, but hardly a close attention to details.

There are certain values to which we adhere as a group bound together by an overarching culture. One of those values is a firm rejection of torture as a means of achieving collective purposes. By torture we mean the infliction of unnecessary pain, pain beyond what is required to achieve those purposes, whatever they may be—the discovery of a terrorist's hidden bomb, the eliciting of a confession. These are deontological values, but they do meet some utilitarian considerations at their extreme (but not in criminal punishments). The thumb-screw and the rack are not to be used to coerce confessions; nor should the pains of imprisonment be used to punish criminality if lesser pains (or imprisonment of lesser duration) can achieve the same socially justified aim.

Is public opinion an appropriate determinant of what pain is reasonably necessary for this purpose? One cannot have absorbed the lessons of the twentieth century and believe that it is. The power of political leadership in pursuit of popular support by relentless and unscrupulous means has surely and frequently been demonstrated. Likewise, in relation to the punishment of crime, a public misled by false statistics, sensational and selective sound bites, and political leaders seeking votes is plain to see.

War after war are seen as necessary and clearly justified by the populaces on both sides of the conflict. Similarly, criminal punishments of obviously excessive brutality, inflicting grossly excessive pain—crucifixion, breaking on the wheel, flogging, and on and on—in their day attracted and held mass popular support.

If popularity is the justification of a punishment, we are

indeed lost. Surely, it is the task of the collective, the group, the government, functioning with dispassionate but firm values, to define what deliberate infliction of pain is appropriate to the punishment of a member of the group. This is a moral task on which polls may be relevant, but must not be determinative.

Happily, that moral task properly undertaken brings in its wake a change in public opinion. As leadership defines criminal punishments with rational balance, that balance comes to influence public opinion to its acceptance. Hence capital punishment is now to be found among Western industrialized countries only in the United States, where it is now under serious attack and is unlikely to be part of the armamentarium of punishment for many more decades.

Thus, the beginning of an answer to our query why prison conditions merit attention is to be found in the fact that the criminal justice system exercises the greatest power that a state can legally use against its citizens. Consequently, a prison regime defines the razor edge between power and freedom, authority and autonomy. *Quis custodiet custodes?* becomes even more probing when extended to who will keep the prison keepers, who will control the ultimate controllers? The answer spreads governments over a wide range, from systematic torturers to tolerant democracies in which even prisoners retain many protections of citizenship.

Many philosophers and reflective politicians have appreciated that reality and have suggested that the treatment of the convicted criminal is a sound barometer to the civilization of a society. Churchill was an exemplar of this affirmation: "The mood and temper of the public with regard to the treatment of crime and criminals is one of the most unfailing tests of the civilization of any country." This may well be so, but why? A greater man, the greatest of men, who had been speaking a few moments earlier of visiting prisons, put the same point more powerfully: "What you do to the least of these, you do unto me."

Returning to the secular, Sir Owen Dixon, Chief Justice of the Australian High Court, a judge I greatly admired, as did virtually all lawyers who knew his work, offered me an answer. He said that when sentencing men in the dock, they often seemed to him very much like himself. Few of us can muster that degree of empathy, but we understand the point. We are all so very much alike, such weak and only occasionally strong vessels, little of human frailty is outside our understanding. There are a few outliers, but only a few. So, when devising prison conditions, you should devise them for yourself. That does not mean you should be self-indulgent. You should consider not only yourself but also how you are bound by the realities of the society in which you live and of the fact that prisons in the last resort exist *faux de mieux*—because we cannot think of anything better to do with a criminal than by imprisonment to make him feel our disapproval and our fear of him and others like him.

The belief is widespread in the United States today that the Reverend Sydney Smith had it right in 1822, though he and his words are not widely remembered. In his view, prison should be "a place of punishment from which men recoil with horror—a place of real suffering, painful to the memory, terrible to the imagination . . . a place of sorrow and wailing, which should be entered with horror and quitted with earnest resolution never to return to such misery; with that deep impression, in short, of the evil which breaks out in perpetual warning and exhortation to others." (Sydney Smith, *On the Management of Prisons, Essays*, Wardle, Locke & Co., London, pp. 226, 232.) In short, "horror" and "misery" will deter convicts and citizens at large from committing crimes. And, if not, the convicts at least will reap what they have sown.

By no great contrast, sympathetic friends, those who share my interest in improving prison conditions, and in providing academic, psychological, and vocational training programs in prison, often rest their case for these developments on the likelihood of thus reducing recidivism. And, if not, at least they have done their best to help wrongdoers become rightdoers.

Part 4

CONTEMPORARY LESSONS
FROM MACONOCHIE'S EXPERIMENT

M aconochie's many writings and the regime he brought to Norfolk Island are replete with ideas relevant to contemporary sentencing, prison, and release practices. He favored indeterminate sentences rather than fixed sentences, he recommended, and in part implemented, a marks system to measure the prisoner's progress toward release from prison, and he urged a system of graduated release and aftercare of prisoners to resettle them in the community.

What then remains of Maconochie's great penal experiment? Does his apparent failure have lessons for us, nearly two centuries later, in our continuing confusion about the proper role of punishment and the prison? Maconochie's principal biographer, Sir John Barry, had no doubt of the answer to that question, writing that "[Maconochie] formulated the conceptions on which modern penology is based, and he put them into practical operation" (J. V. Barry, *The Life and Death of John Price*, Melbourne University Press, 1964, p. 21). In support of this evaluation, Barry suggested that Maconochie's writings and the spread of knowledge of his work on Norfolk Island and in Birmingham prison had a profound effect in the United States, being widely accepted and advocated by the then powerful prison reform movement and its American Prison Association. Barry therefore concluded that "his influence lives on."

That was indeed the accepted view in 1964 when Barry wrote, but a great deal has changed since then, much for the worse, so that the value and truth of Maconochie's ideas merit critical contemporary analysis.

Fixed or Indeterminate Sentences and "Good Time"

> When a man keeps the key of his own prison he is soon persuaded to fit it to the lock

Maconochie's phrase, that the prisoner should keep the key to his own cell, is an idea that resonates both as "behavioral conditioning" and as "the indeterminate sentence" through twentieth-century psychology and criminology. When he advanced the idea in the 1830s it was novel to the point of absurdity—and was so seen. They thought him a visionary, out of touch with the realities of the world and human nature. But how could that be? After all, he had captained ships, fought well in wars, had himself been a prisoner of war, was highly regarded as an intellectual geographer, came from a good family, and was a close friend of England's hero of the Arctic, Sir John Franklin. The general inclination was to esteem him highly, but to recognize that on one subject, the convict regime, he seemed to be a sentimental fool.

Having the prisoner hold the key to his cell was not quite what Maconochie actually proposed and what he in fact did on Norfolk Island. He opposed the typical convict regime, dominated by tight control backed up by deterrent brutality, though he had, of course, ordered the flogging and hanging of sailors when he captained ships. And when he governed Norfolk Island he imposed the same severe corporal sanctions for what were regarded as serious breaches of prison discipline or capital offenses, but he did insist on fair proof of the disciplinary offense and did try to eliminate punitive brutality based on the personal animus of guards. So what was novel?

The then dominant opinion, and one perhaps still holding sway in the halls of our legislatures, is that the criminal does not change for the better by educative or training methods, but changes only by fear of the painful or terminal consequences of misbehavior. He can advance toward conformity to law only by the threat of condign punishment. The transportation of convicts to the United States and later to Australia carried no element of positive conditioning. You served your term of years being worked as a convict for the state or as an indentured laborer for a free citizen. When the term was completed, you were to be freed. During your term the whip, the lash, and the noose would ensure your obedience.

There had been cracks in this wall of deterrence and inexorable punishment. The ticket-of-leave had been developed before Maconochie made an extended use of it on Norfolk Island. Some indentured convicts escaped their masters, were not vigorously chased and not recaptured, and began ordinary and productive lives away from wherever they had been held— in the United States by fleeing to the burgeoning cities, in Australia by fleeing to the "bush" where some became "bushrangers."

Maconochie developed his "Marks System" as a means of precisely rewarding the prisoner for his industry and behavior and withdrawing the reward equally precisely for misbehavior and sloth. An island ticket-of-leave and your own small house and farm were a positive incentive when sufficient marks had been earned and, though this was more hoped for than regularly achieved, a Sydney ticket-of-leave to be earned thereafter. The end result would depend on the original sentence imposed on the convict. If it was transportation for life, that could not be changed except by royal clemency; if it was transportation for a term of years, at the end of that term the convict could stay in Australia, or return to England or Ireland, or go elsewhere, but tickets-of-leave could not influence that term.

Maconochie thus advocated, and in part implemented, a system of positive and negative conditioning for prisoners in advance of anything then suggested. He did not believe in the perfectability of man, but he certainly did believe in man's improvability given appropriate encouragement and hope. Avoiding breach of prison rules, working hard, being neat and orderly, cooperating with your fellow prisoners in their work and in their living conditions could earn you a defined quantum of marks that would be the currency of increased integers of autonomy in your daily life. You would know where you stood with this currency, how to earn more, and how to lose some or all of it. Quite precisely, this is positive and negative conditioning measured by "marks."

In 1840, the death penalty was described as the "primary" punishment; sentences to prison or to transportation were described as "secondary" punishments. Maconochie's writings focused on secondary punishments. His view was that none of these should be "time defined," but all should be "indeterminate," with their conclusion dependent on the completion of a defined amount of work and on the prisoner's behavior during his confinement for work—thus "work defined" rather than "time defined." There was the added and important gloss that by the accumulation of "marks" measuring progress toward completion of the allotted work, the prisoner should gain improved living conditions including a "ticket-of-leave" so that his work could continue in the community rather than in prison.

The intervening century and a half has produced a much greater diversity in noncapital punishments, including fines, probation, intensive probation, halfway houses (in and out), community service (which would have held great attraction for Maconochie), compulsory drug and other treatment programs, and a wide variety of prison settings ranging from lightly secured open prisons to the current cruelties of "supermax" cellblocks and prisons. Nevertheless we still have a great deal to learn from Maconochie's principles.

People change. They learn. They "grow up." Most learning and emotional growth is self-motivated and self-induced. It requires the rest of us not to get in the way, to facilitate, but not try to impose change. Most delinquent and criminal adolescents in all societies become productive, conforming citizens on their own, if they are allowed to, once the fires of youth subside. Certainly they can be helped to learn and to change. A brief experience of living behind bars induces compliance in a few, while another few are peculiarly resistant to the threats and realities of punishment. Meanwhile, for the greater incarcerated mass, prison renders them more rebellious to authority, more criminous, since the very essence of prison—absolute control and repression of individuality—is criminogenic. That the majority pf people released from prison do not return is a testament to human adaptability.

Maconochie's "Marks System" was built on views like those. It relied on each individual's affection for autonomy and self-direction. Thus, "work obligations" rather than "time obligations" should define punishments for crime, since the criminal could do nothing about the passage of time, except wait, while if a quantum of work and good behavior measured his punishment he could actively participate in its termination. Hence even in his cell he should be given work to do, if he so wished, to expedite his graduation toward increasing autonomy.

For these reasons criminal punishments must, as Maconochie saw it, be forward looking toward reformation and not backward looking toward the infliction of deserved suffering or terrorization to virtue. And, since he had little faith in deterrence as a means of controlling criminal behavior, his system took shape. For the crime, impose a prison "work term" appropriate to the gravity of the crime, the criminal's intent and circumstances, and other matters relevant to sentencing, to be served in the accumulation of marks to measure progress toward completion of the punishment. But then freedom must be tested in the laboratory of the world and not the unreal world of the prison; hence supervision of conformity after release until full autonomy was achieved and free citizenship regained.

The idea has great surface appeal, but it confronts the formidable obstacle that we lack ability to predict human behavior except in the form of a statement of probability, now called "risk assessment," which means that any prediction in any given case has a defined likelihood of being wrong. In the modern world of political realities, no one wishes to accept responsibility for an erroneous prediction that the prisoner will no longer commit crime if released, when crime is certain to recur with more or less frequency among those predicted as safe, because public condemnation of whoever allowed the release is highly likely.

Nevertheless, it seems a good idea: Assist, train, and observe the prisoner until he is ready for an increased dose of freedom and another and another until he can in similar controlled and assisted fashion be eased back into society as a contributing, law-abiding member. The problem for all such judgments is that they are as a general rule beyond our competence. Certainly such ideas can only be pursued with the prisoner's cooperation and, given the urge of all to be free of prison, even the prisoner himself may not know whether he really is pursuing the goal of self-regeneration and rehabilitation or whether he is merely going along with the system because it is the easier course to follow and leads more expeditiously to freedom. Human behavior is a product of the confluence of personality, community, and circumstance; their interaction eludes us in many cases. So even if we can train and observe and assist a person until we are confident he will not commit another crime of violence, all that we can really state about him is that there is a defined chance of his conformity to law, but there is also, in virtually every case, a much lower chance of his further serious criminality, and as inexorable statistical matter there is thus the certainty that in some cases our prediction of safety will fail. Like the croupier, we can state the risks, but not where the ball will fall. Politicians and parole boards dislike this game and its certain losses; the only figure in the criminal justice system who should properly consider such predictions, bounded of course by the gravity of the harm the prisoner has already encompassed, is the judge. The judge should be assisted in this task, but the ultimate responsibility should be that of the judge.

Maconochie chose between a "time sentence" and a "work and behavior sentence" and insisted that prison punishments should be "indeterminate." His error lay in choosing at all; he should have combined these ideas into a "time sentence" (a fixed minimum and maximum term imposed by a judge) within which a prisoner's work and behavior in prison could determine the date of release from prison. A judge is the best qualified and best politically protected member of society to define an upper limit of time for a prison term based on the gravity of the crime, the intent or recklessness of the criminal, and many other circumstances of the crime, the victim, and the criminal, including the statistical likelihood of the prisoner's future criminal behavior. The judge is in no position to predict reformation, but it is entirely proper for him or her to take into account the different degrees of risk of future criminality by convicted criminals. Nor is the warden or superintendent of the prison, or a parole board, in a much better position than the judge to achieve predictive foreknowledge of the later behavior of the released prisoner. But they are in a much better position to gradually influence that later behavior by increasing graduated doses of autonomy within the prison or prison system until the prison term expires.

Criminals can and do learn in prison. We can influence what and how they learn. Reformation as a purpose of a criminal punishment is a good and achievable concept. This does not mean that it can inexorably be achieved. It does mean that with reformative purposes and educative (in a broad sense) opportunities we can reduce the occurrence of future crime by a released convicted criminal.

That having been said, one confronts the next set of problems in indeterminate punishments that beset Maconochie and all who have followed his precepts. Who actually measures fitness for the next step toward freedom, and what are the criteria for judging that issue?

As prison guards, Maconochie had soldiers under the orders of their officers. I doubt that many of the officers wanted to be on the island or wanted the duties that they had been given. And the same was probably true of the soldiers who had, after all, been drafted or had volunteered as soldiers, not as prison guards. By contrast, the modern prison administrator has as his staff a group of men and women who have sought this employment and have received, in some form or other, a training program and experience to help them in their work. But then or now, the problem of measuring the individual prisoner's diligence and conformity remains intractable. Different guards have different perspectives of the prisoner. Generally speaking, for the prisoner to be apparently submissive, polite, occasionally jocular, and in no way to stand out will generate the optimum assessment of work well done and discipline observed.

Thus, in practice, measurement of "good behavior" is a product of avoiding observed and recorded "bad behavior." Given the disproportionate ratio of prisoners to guards, it can hardly be otherwise. So, for the most part, the indeterminate sentence becomes a sentence with time off for the avoidance of a disciplinary record. Maconochie could not observe the diligence and behavior of each prisoner each day, nor can any parole board. All that they have to consider in relation to each prisoner's prison life is the impression the prisoner has made on various staff members and the individual record of avoidance of disciplinary incidents.

When parole boards try to avoid this reality, and attempt to make individual-based assessments of fitness for release, they tend to turn the prison into a school of dramatic art in which the chaplain is enlisted by terpsichorean efforts of the prisoner to testify to the prisoner's sudden and complete conversion to religious rectitude, as if on the road to Damascus, or the trade instructor to affirm the prisoner's extraordinary efforts to master the trade he teaches. The blunt truth is that at the time of sentencing as good a prediction as to when the prisoner can be safely released can be made as at any later time during confinement. Those sentenced to long terms are exceptions, most of whom will pass through "criminal menopause" during their late thirties or early forties, aging out of their criminous proclivities. When any prisoner *ought* to be released is a different matter, turning on the gravity of the crime, the background and intent of the criminal, and the prisoner's avoidance of disciplinary infractions meriting the loss of "good time."

Apart from the intractable difficulty of predicting human behavior, there are two further practical impediments to the contemporary adoption of Maconochie's ideas concerning the proper release date: the lack of work in prison and the problem of "time off for good behavior," known in prison as "good time."

There are exceptions, but the prevailing condition in the crowded prisons of the world is a scarcity of useful work. Penal administrators, guards, and prisoners generally agree on the need for useful work for prisoners to do (not make-work, not using ten men to do the work of one). Idle hands indeed fill the devil's workshop. Prisoners with nothing to do, nothing to burn off youthful energy, will often get into mischief or worse.

With considerable success, private economic interests and trade unions have blocked the availability of useful work in prisons on the grounds, respectively, that it is unfair competition and that it denies jobs to people who have committed no crime. The idea of a full-wages prison, with the prisoner paying his share of the costs of his imprisonment as well as compensating his victim has been widely discussed and tried in some European prisons, but in the United States, with a few tiny exceptions, it meets unremitting hostility. Thus, idleness and its attendant problems for both keepers and kept remain the dominant condition.

Production of useful goods by prisoners for "state use" has been accepted to a degree, so that the Federal Bureau of Prisons has an excellent work program for many of its prisoners owing to the huge extent of the federal government market (including the Department of Defense), but the states have no comparable market and idleness pervades state prisons. For Maconochie's charges there was no lack of work and the same is true in most contemporary minimum security and farm prisons, but the bulk of those behind bars have no work to do. Nor have they other than random and scarce access to educational or vocational training programs besides the most basic. Thus, diligence in work or in educational programs could be no guide to their fitness for release. Of course, refusal to work or laziness at what work was found for them could be used as such a guide, but essentially a work-defined sentence as distinct from a time-defined sentence makes no contemporary sense.

The second problem is that of "time off for good behavior" or "good time." As the forces of experience and analysis push us away from indeterminate sentencing, the question of good time confronts the prison administrator.

Even though the criminal law of course runs in prison as elsewhere, and a prisoner can be tried, convicted, and further sentenced for a statutory offense committed while in prison, those running prisons argue that it is necessary, if discipline is to be preserved, to provide some part of each prisoner's duration of confinement to be under the control of the correctional authorities. The withdrawal of privileges and periods of punitive segregation are insufficient, it is widely believed, to preserve discipline, certainly in a maximum security prison. This argument has prevailed in the United States, and "good time" is under the control of the prison authorities throughout our prisons. But good time turns out to be, in practice, not the demonstration of good behavior but success in avoiding the commission and detection of bad behavior.

In cases of exceptional virtue when a crisis occurs and a prisoner leaps into the breach, good behavior can be noted and rewarded, if appropriate, even by a gubernatorial or a presidential pardon. But, in the run-of-the-mill crowded prison, good behavior is transmogrified into the avoidance of bad behavior, so that the avoidance of disciplinary offenses or of observed and reported hostility to authority is the measure of good behavior. The harder question then becomes how serious must the infraction be to justify loss of good time. But the existence of this power is not seriously in present doubt. The harder question is what are the appropriate procedures for establishing the "serious" disciplinary offense.

There is a gloss on this of considerable importance. The issue of "good time" presses even on those who advocate fixed-term sentencing. When a parole board is in place dealing with indeterminate sentences, prison misbehavior becomes an important factor in the exercise of the board's releasing decision. Absent indeterminacy in sentencing, the prison administration, with reason, argues that it lacks an important weapon in the task of maintaining order and discipline within the prison. As a result, "good time" is an element of all imprisonment in the United States, and generally throughout the Western world. "Good time" is obviously a euphemism for "bad time"; it says to the prisoner: If you break the prison rules you may be punished not only by withdrawal of privileges or by a period in segregation, but we may also take some or all of your "good time" from you, effectively prolonging the time you will remain behind bars.

Since 1987, the U.S. Congress has required federal prisoners to serve at least 85 percent of their sentences and, in 1994, extended that mandate to "violent" prisoners confined by the states. In exchange for thus limiting good time, the states received federal funds for building new prisons and hiring more guards. Most states fell into line, while others have enthusiastically extended the good time limitation to all prisoners, or have eliminated good time altogether, so that generally in America good time is now limited to 15 percent of the imposed sentences. Given the Draconian length of sentences now in fashion, except for relatively minor felonies, good time has dwindled in importance, except as a factor in prison overcrowding and, of course, to the prisoner.

Good time is not much discussed in the literature on prisons (for an excellent analysis and a bibliography, see James B. Jacobs, "Sentencing by Prison Personnel: Good Time," 30 *U.C.L.A. L. Rev.* 216–70, 1982), which is surprising considering the extent of arbitrary power it gives to the prison administrator; power, in effect, to sentence a prisoner to further imprisonment other than on proof of a crime with only the flimsiest of due process protections.

And there is a further problem with good time. Should it "vest" year by year or should it just hang there like a darkening cloud over every prisoner until he or she is released? Suppose a prisoner's period of possible good time in a five-year sentence is one year. When he has served three and a half years, the threat of a loss of good time is a vastly different threat from the first day of his sentence. Experienced prison administrators know, as do some guards and prisoners, that the periods of greatest emotional difficulty for the prisoner occur early in the sentence and again during the few months before a parole hearing or a good-time release date. High expectations have been built up; it will be so wonderful to be free again. And yet these are also the times when the threat of a breach of prison discipline and consequent further imprisonment looms large. A guard or a fellow prisoner, if he wishes, can get the prisoner into trouble and thus long defer his release, possibly for years, through relatively unsupervised sentencing to prison by prison authorities. It gives largely unregulated power to other prisoners, who can, without much trouble, "set up" or involve another prisoner in a disciplinary offense. Further, as we have seen, it gives a huge measure of power to prison guards, for it is they who file the disciplinary reports that reviewing supervisors rarely question.

The solution is clear: Good time should vest; that is, in our hypothetical five-year sentence of which one year is "good time," after one year in prison the amount of good time you can lose should be reduced to nine months, after two years, to six months, and so on. A powerful case for this reform was made by the then Director of the Federal Bureau of Prisons, Norman Carlson, in 1982 before the House Judiciary Committtee. It has attracted neither widespread refutation nor adoption. It is a manifestly just reform that should be universally adopted.

As a result, the judge is in as good a position as the parole board to predict later criminal conduct. Some flexibility in the release date must be given to the prison authorities to assist them to run an orderly prison, but that flexibility should be confined to deferment of the first judicially authorized release date by serious disciplinary offenses, not enlarged to adjust between conformity and apparent achievement.

Given these several limitations, it is hard to see what the "Marks System" contributed to Norfolk Island. Very little, I think, beyond instilling in the prisoner a slender hope of eventual freedom. Yet the life of the prison changed dramatically, from pervasive brutality to relative peace and order. For two reasons, I suggest: first, Maconochie's empathy and humaneness as superintendent that I have tried to depict in the earlier fact–fiction about his work on the island; second, because of his adherence to the implicit contract between keeper and kept in all prisons. This idea of an implicit contract between keepers and kept is a more difficult and less understood concept.

The typical prison runs by consent of the imprisoned. Within the walls, if prisoners are allowed to associate, they hold the overwhelming physical power. The walls can be manned with guns, and this will effectively define the limits of prisoners' power. Alternatively, the prisoners can be held isolated from one another by "lockdown" or by a supermax prison, and this shifts power back to the authorities. These exceptions apart, the general pattern of staff–prisoner relationships is defined by the understanding that they share a mutual goal—a smooth running, orderly prison. Almost all prisoners for their part, contrary to popular opinion, will "go along to get along"; disruption, violence, and chaos are as ill received by them as by members of society. Most staff then see fit not to subject prisoners to arbitrary, purposeless, or needlessly humiliating rules. An unspoken, implicit, but quite real "contract" emerges and produces a mainly peaceful prison, though, of course, in any large group of men there will be rogues who will break the rules of that contract and are, in the eyes of the prison administration and the bulk of the prisoners, properly to be punished. Only undeserved or wildly disproportionate punishment causes wide resentment Problems of overcrowding as well as gang and ethnic hostilities may to a degree frustrate this implied contract, but nevertheless it widely exists and certainly existed from 1840 to 1844 on Norfolk Island.

Maconochie's overarching approach to governing a penal colony embodied adherence to this implied contract. A superintendent who moved man to man throughout the entire settlement, talking and listening, and not imposing any merely humiliating rules on those subject to his charge. A sense of understanding among the prisoners that, given their circumstances, the administration was directed toward an enlargement and not a diminution of their freedom. A willingness by the administration to trust a prisoner, without abandoning a willingness to punish him subject to decent proof of breach of that trust. A sense of pervading fairness, at least as a sincere objective. These were the qualities, and not the "Marks System," that turned the island from hell to a peaceful settlement for four of its otherwise barbarous years.

How do lessons like this transfer to the modern prison? I argue that the judge should at sentencing set the outer limit of detention subject to good time (whatever it generally is). Thereafter, prison authorities should control gradual extensions of freedom within the prison (with the release date deferrable for established and serious disciplinary offenses). After release the prisoner should be under the control of the aftercare authorities for a defined maximum term. These curt submissions require some elaboration.

In the late 1970s, we were gradually moving toward implementing those submissions. At the end of the century, we have almost entirely abandoned them and instead rely on severity as a deterrent, and lengthy incapacitation in prison as an end in itself.

In the 1970s, the Federal Parole Board had developed parole prediction tables by which the members of the board, the prison authorities, and the prisoner could calculate the prisoner's presumptive release date to which the board would adhere except for unusual and well-considered reasons having relevance to the particular case. The prisoner would then be released not to the community but to a CCC, a Community Control Center, to live by night and on weekends while he went out to find work or to go to work for a period before a further enlargement of his freedom. This sensible practice, fulfilling the essence of Maconochie's ideas, died in the late 1970s in the wake of rising crime rates and a burgeoning number of prisoners, and after widespread acceptance of the idea that "nothing works" to reform prisoners. That, and disparities in how much time prisoners served for identical crimes, disparities that too often followed racial lines, led to fixed terms of imprisonment replacing indeterminate terms. The political left wanted short, fixed sentences followed by ample parole supervision. The political right wanted long, fixed terms with few opportunities for parole. The right won. It is time we rediscovered that our current sentencing practices and prison and release practices are out of tune with fiscal probity, justice, and the basic principles of human dignity on which this country was founded.

To conclude this discussion of indeterminacy, let me take Maconochie's ideas and filter them through the experience and literature of the intervening century and a half and try to distill their current worth as a guide to punishing and imprisoning criminals. Let us set aside problems of compensating victims, of restorative justice, of drug treatment programs, of probation, intensive probation, halfway houses, and the rich non-incarcerative sentences available to many judges, and let us concentrate on what is fair and effective for what should be the ultimate criminal punishment—imprisonment.

Both in deciding whether to use prison as a punishment in a given case and in setting the terms of imprisonment if that is the sentence, the judge is and should remain the central figure. If prison is decided upon, the judge should set the maximum term, the date of parole release (subject to time off for good behavior, which is usually legislatively prescribed as a proportion of the sentence), and the maximum duration of parole (subject, of course, to the commission of a further crime during that period). These two dates should not be subject to control by the prison authorities or by the parole or aftercare authorities. The maximum term available to the judge in the case before him or her will be limited by the statute defining the offense, and better practice will have installed a legislatively or gubernatorially appointed sentencing commission to guide but not bind the judge in the exercise of this sentencing discretion, with an appeal against sentence allowed to the prisoner should the judge be more severe than the guidelines provide and an appeal by the prosecutor should the judge be less firm than the guidelines direct. This requires the judge to give reasons for the sentence when it lies outside the guidelines.

The prison authorities have a discretion to exercise that has nearly as much impact on the prisoner as the sentence itself. They determine the conditions within the prison system in which the prisoner will be held, from maximum to minimum security, from a restricted to an ample educative program, from make-work to real work, from a relaxed environment to a maximum security lockdown. And the prisoner's behavior, measured for these purposes by the guards and the prison authorities, should allow his or her advance to increasing autonomy through these stages after reception to prison as if climbing a ladder. The highest rung on this ladder should be a halfway house, something like the CCC, where the prisoner resides in the early days of release from prison and goes out daily to work or find work.

Graduated Release Procedures and Aftercare

The last stage in Maconochie's "Marks System" was the requirement of graduated release procedures, including supervision within the community, leading to ultimate freedom; but Maconochie was, of course, fundamentally limited in developing a graduated release procedure beyond a certain stage. Although he did have control over island tickets-of-leave and could check the prisoner's continuing diligence and conformity to law while out of prison walls on the island, he could not control a graduated return to society in New South Wales or elsewhere. All he could do was to recommend it, and his recommendations were rarely accepted and almost randomly rejected.

Few would disagree with the desirability of graduated release for the prisoner. An unconditional and unplanned opening of the gates to a hostile world is a recipe for recidivism. Some pre-release planning and action, some support in post-prison housing, some guidance to a world of gainful employment is in the interests of the community and of the prisoner. Some degree of control in the early release period is also well advised. There is little disagreement on such matters, but little is done nowadays in practice to implement them. Like the jails and the courts and the punishment/correctional system, the prisoner aftercare programs have been overrun by the numbers supposedly under their care, by lack of funds and facilities, and by public suspicion and political opposition to their very existence.

In the year 2000, about 600,000 prisoners were released from federal and state prisons. This takes no account of the millions processed through jails. Do these 600,000 spell a likely measureable increase in the crime rate? Probably not. The numbers to be so released have been high since our "get tough on crime" policy took hold in the last quarter of the twentieth century, and release help and control have been largely constant or decreasing, except in relation to sexual offenders toward whom there has been an effort to greatly extend controls, and even through a form of civil commitment after release to further incarcerate them, though not to help.

Revocations of parole or of release conditions have been a steadily increasing proportion of those each year entering state prisons, so that in several states they now exceed the number of those coming to prison by court sentence. Overall, the crime rate moves to lower rates, but the rate of misery for the releasees and for those who have retained affection for them steadily grows. Most who enter prison lack adequate education, employable skills, and family supports; most have doubts at one level or another of their self-worth. In our overcrowded prisons there has been little attempt to remedy these deficiencies. The increasing length of sentences has meant that they emerge older than they used to and therefore less criminous, but the wasted intervening prison years have often exacerbated rather than diminished the personality and family problems with which they arrived in prison.

Maconochie would have none of it. Nor should we. And he charted the path that should be followed: a pre-release program within the prison as the prison term draws to a close, a halfway house release for those who do not have a welcoming home to go to, some support in seeking employment—overall, the gradual reduction of controls and the gradual extension of supported autonomy.

To achieve these aims, the parole or aftercare authorities should tailor the conditions of the released prisoner's life in the community to the realities of the needs for a law-abiding and productive resettlement, and relax their controls as progress is made. They should be reluctant indeed to impose and enforce conditions on that release that are not essential to the prisoner's becoming a law-abiding citizen; there is, in effect, a subsidiary implicit contract that can be broken by excessive paternalism or insufficient appropriate support. These ideas still seem utopian, as they must have to Maconochie; but that does not deny their worth.

"The Worst of the Worst"

Norfolk Island took those who having been convicted as felons in England or Ireland were sent to the Australian penal colonies and there committed further crimes for which they were further transported. There were also a few soldiers who were convicted of criminal or military offenses in New South Wales and Van Diemen's Land who were sent to Norfolk Island, but the bulk of prisoners were doubly convicted convicts—in the eyes of the time, the worst of the worst, fit to live neither in their homeland nor in a convict settlement where free settlers also lived.

The modern parallel is the supermax prison. Terrible things have been happening as a result of the criminal justice system of the United States turning too far away from the ideas that motivated Maconochie. Instead of requiring each maximum security prison to handle its own disciplinary problems, there has been created a pattern of "supermax" prisons spreading fast across the entire country. It is not far-fetched to see them as the modern equivalent of Norfolk Island, the place to which those unfit to live even in a maximum security prison will be banished.

This deep end of the prison system raises similar problems to those that Maconochie confronted in 1840, with the distinction that the passage of years has led us to impose a degree of sensory deprivation on prisoners that Norfolk Island never attained. Norfolk Island may lead us in physical tortures but we are far ahead in psychological tortures. John Price and Major Childs seems to be our model wardens rather than Alexander Maconochie.

The impetus to the creation of supermax prisons was the killing in 1983 of two guards by prisoners in the maximum security section of the federal prison at Marion in Illinois. Thereafter the Federal Bureau of Prisons built the supermax at Florence, Colorado, and California created its supermax at Pelican Bay. Texas, Virginia, and other states followed suit, and it is unclear precisely how many such institutions and special control sections of institutions now exist, but they pervade prison regimes in most if not all states.

Their characteristics are similar. They provide near complete isolation of the prisoner from other prisoners as well as very scant contact between prisoner and guard. Commonly the prisoner spends at least twenty-three hours of every day and on many days twenty-four hours alone in a cell, denied telephone calls to family, and denied any program that might help him refashion his life. These conditions are designed for prisoners who have been disruptive or violent while in prison and for whom it is thought that ordinary disciplinary and segregative controls are inadequate.

These are long-term institutions with confinement measured in years, not months. The architectural and technological design of such institutions reduces the need for verbal interaction between prisoner and staff and eliminates other than remote shouting from communication between prisoner and prisoner. Further, supermax prisons are characterized by scant or non-existent programmed activities. No work opportunities are offered. Law library, religious, and educational materials are, where available, typically delivered to cells and if there any substance abuse treatments available or vocational training or educational materials, they are provided through centrally controlled television or by correspondence. The hour the prisoner is allowed out on some days is spent in a solitary yard not much bigger than his cell, but often with a view of the sky or the outside world that is lacking in the cell.

Dynamics of domination, control, subordination, and submission are fundamentally different in supermax prisons from those in regular maximum security prisons, even when the latter are on "lockdown" with the congregate life of the prison no longer permitted. The basic difference between the two regimes is that in the supermax one prisoner cannot communicate with another in a normal manner. The ensuing near-totality of sensory deprivation is no minor loss; it can and does result in a buildup of rage and paranoia with commensurate psychological distintegration. Other distinctions flow from the separateness of many supermax prisons from the rest of the prison system.

Working as a guard in a supermax is very different from working as one in a maximum security prison. Everything in

a supermax turns on the punitive isolation of the inmate, producing a culture based on unremitting guard-to-prisoner hostility. That is not so in a well-run maximum security prison,
where a wide variety of staff–inmate interactions exist. Supermax is a culture unleavened by normal relaxed contacts between prisoner and guard or prisoner and prisoner as exist to
a degree in all maximum security prisons.

The justification for this extent of control and sensory deprivation in the supermax prison is that this is both the best
way of handling some incorrigibly dangerous prisoners and
that by removing these worst apples from the barrel of the
prison, the barrel will be a safer place in which to live. Neither
of these justifications has been measured; they are supported
only by selected anecdotal evidence and the naked assertions
of some prison officials.

The supermax frenzy still remains a phenomenon confined to
the United States, though there is now such an institution built
in South Africa. The United Kingdom has tested some close supervision centers and has then examined the whole question in
the Woolf Report (Home Office, 1991, "Prison Disturbances
April 1990. Report of an Inquiry by the Rt. Hon. Lord Justice
Woolf and His Honour Judge Stephen Tumim" in 1456, February 1991. London HMSO.) and has rejected the supermax.

A central question in relation to every supermax prison is
the processes of selection of candidates for transfer from maximum security to the supermax. Again, the comparison with
Norfolk Island may be helpful. There is no doubt that in 1840
there were convicts in the antipodean colonies who were in
violent and determined conflict with the authorities. It does
not seem to me at all inappropriate to have sent them on to
Norfolk Island where larger controls were available, and where

they could not inflict suffering on the civilian population. Of course, for conditions on the island, the Maconochie regime is on all accounts to be preferred to the brutality that preceded and followed his period.

The selection of those to be sent to Norfolk Island was decided by the courts in the colonies, which gave a substantial measure of due process hearing to the accused. By contrast, the selection of prisoners for transfer to the supermax prisons in the United States is not done by courts, but is a process of classification, in practice within the unfettered control of the relevant prison managers. Those who have studied supermax prisons agree that there is a real danger of overdetermination of those suitable for such control, that the persistent nuisances and troublemakers are included with the demonstrated high-risk, violent prisoners.

Likewise with the question of duration of detention in a supermax. The prisoner will be held until he demonstrates his suitability to be returned to a maximum security prison. But how can he so demonstrate in the conditions imposed within a supermax? In practice only by a rigid avoidance of the slightest disciplinary offense, such as not returning his food tray through the slot in his cell door in a timely fashion, or not being in any way disrespectful to the guards on the rare occasions when he is spoken to. As a result, unaccountable prison bureaucrats decide who goes to supermax and how long he stays. Protracted and severe sensory deprivation is imposed without adequate judicial control. It is no surprise that arbitrary power, as Lord Acton affirmed, tends to generate its own misuse.

What would Maconochie's solution be to the present reality of dangerous and difficult-to-handle prisoners? I think the principle he would follow is clear: Impose the least afflictive control necessary in the light of the threat, and let each maximum security prison look after its own troublemakers.

There is simply no need for a supermax prison or a supermax section of a prison in any state prison system. For the extraordinarily rare cases that cannot be handled by prosecution for crime, by punitive segregation, or by transfer to prisons where their outside influences are of no avail, there is the federal supermax at Florence which, as these prisons go, has a defined program and a defined technique of reducing control as the program is followed and is willing to take such rare cases off the hands of state departments on a contract basis.

The present path of increasing the populations of supermax prisons is cruel, expensive, and counterproductive in terms of the prisoner's later behavior in the community. It is unworthy of a nation claiming to be dedicated to human rights, a nation that does not hesitate to chastise other countries when they fall short on that account.

One particularly appalling aspect of the mushroom growth of supermax incarceration is the extent that seriously mentally ill prisoners find themselves subject to this sensory deprivation. There is some argument in the literature whether prisoners deteriorate in the supermax situation of sensory deprivation, but I find it hard to imagine what it must be like for a seriously mentally ill prisoner in a supermax cell at night, isolated from everyone and everything that stimulates life, his half-sleep filled with imaginary conversations and then periods of hallucination, common to the seriously mentally ill, visual and audible stimuli, many of them powerfully threatening, which yet at one distant level he knows not to be there, but are nevertheless very real, and the pain becomes far more than my empathy can reach.

What a contrast to Maconochie's treatment of "Bony," who clearly had become demented by his treatment in Sydney, on Goat Island, and then on Norfolk Island. Maconochie's brilliant idea of the bullocks and Bony's protected peace were followed by regular visits by Maconochie himself, who gave by his presence some sense of human comfort to the battered Bony.

Punishment and the Mentally Ill

Maconochie's handling of Bony leads to reflections on the relationship between mental illness and crime, and the treatment of those two broad categories of people.

During the so-called Dark Ages, awash in magical thinking, "devils" had to be driven out of the body they inhabited. Everyone recognized that truth and took means to conform to its message. Flogging was one way, burning another, to extract the devil from the body and soul it had tried to take over. If the devils invaded animals, then, of course, the biblical direction could be followed and they should be driven over a cliff. Witches were yet a different matter; invariably older and past their childbearing usefulness, they required drowning or burning to eliminate the succubi that possessed them. Despite all these heroic and well-respected efforts, the incidence of devils in human bodies seemed to remain roughly constant.

Later, following the Renaissance, less superstitious explanations of mental illness took hold. There were no devils. Persons previously thought to be possessed by them were now "mad," victims of mental disorders, not hosts to devils. But the infliction of pain continued on the bodies and minds of many who had mental disease. They were shut away in attics or cellars, or in state-run bedlams called lunatic asylums, where they suffered gross cruelties. Quite recently, mental illness has come to be seen as a genetic or biochemical defect in the brain, to be treated by antipsychotic drugs. With that perception, and with some prodding by the U.S. Supreme Court to depopulate mental hospitals, the states in the 1970s all but emptied the back wards of their mental hospitals so that the mentally ill could be chemically treated at outpatient mental health clinics and in the community. The clinics and the community care never appeared. Many thousands of the indigent mentally ill were thrown into the ranks of the homeless or into grossly inadequate shelters. Their untreated illness produced bizarre behavior, troublesome to others and sometimes criminal, so many thousands landed in jail or prison, where they received inadequate care, or none at all beyond solitary confinement, massive doses of tranquilizers to "quiet them down," and sometimes four-point restraints when they refused to be still.

When Maconochie took over the governance of Norfolk Island, he very likely had a substantial proportion of his convict population suffering what would now be diagnosed as serious mental illness, but who were then regarded as possessed of a free will that, sufficently engaged, could remedy their frequently disturbing and sometimes threatening behavior.

Psychotherapeutic efforts have changed, but imposed suffering still continues. Prison is not the place for a seriously mentally ill criminal. Jail is not the place for a mentally ill vagrant. By and large, those propositions are agreed to in principle but not in practice.

Divide the world of the seriously mentally ill into two parts—clearly a superficial division, but bear with it. One group will be those who are withdrawn into their own fantasy life, deeply depressed, catatonic, passive, and unaggressive; they do not normally find their way to prisons. They are indeed the residue of the seriously mentally ill to be found in our mental hospitals, or homeless on the streets, or in jails, or scraping by in marginal circumstances. They did not manifest behavior that would bring them to prison. It is the others, the aggressive, the bizarre, the acting out mentally ill who become prison inmates. And, of that group who reach prison, a high proportion have difficulty living there. Their symptoms grow more bizarre and threatening, and they become subject to prison punishments and to transfer to the most controlled prison environments—in 1840 to Norfolk Island, in 2002 to a supermax.

It would be wrong to see this result as somehow the fault of the felony-sentencing courts or of the prison administration. The psychiatrist or the trained social worker look very differently at the behavior of the seriously mentally ill from the legislator or the judge or the prison administrator. The former search for the pressures that precipitate the criminal behavior; the latter respond to the fact of the criminal behavior and place high values on retribution and deterrence. And if the criminal's behavior becomes excessively bizarre, the legislator, the judge, and the warden often suspect that malingering, not mental illness, is the cause.

Little allowance is made for the mentally ill convict in prison. One perspective is that of the prison administrator and the prison guards, the other the perspective of the psychiatrist, psychologist, and social worker; they have different visions of the same behavior and of the same individual. One is primarily punitive, the other primarily treatment oriented. The deeper the prisoner moves into the criminal justice system, the more likely the punitive perspective will dominate. It is difficult to blame prison administrators. Their mission, the same as Maconochie's, is to manage an orderly escape-proof prison for healthy young criminals. Today, after the ballooning of the prison population and proliferation of protracted sentences, prison managers are asked to be warden, chief medical officer, and chief psychiatrist. They must care for sizeable populations of elderly, infirm, and mentally ill prisoners, something they are neither inclined, trained, nor sufficiently funded to do.

In practice, the police officer is often the gatekeeper of this whole issue. He or she sees or is advised of criminal behavior. If that behavior is life threatening or of a felonious kind, the officer will take the offender to the police booking station whether or not he sees or senses serious mental illness in that offender. If that behavior is less threatening or less injurious, and the officer sees or senses serious mental illness, he is at present empowered to take that person to the emergency admitting room of the nearest psychiatric hospital.

In practice only a minority of seriously mentally ill criminals are taken on the latter path, most being thrust along the punitive path. This is no criticism of the police. Their choice is one of considerable difficulty, and there is less administrative burden, less delay, and less uncertainty at the police booking station than at the emergency admitting room.

There are several available remedies to this situation. First, the burden of decision on the police should be lightened by administrative practices at psychiatric emergency rooms. They should either take responsibility for the arrestee from the shoulders of the police officer by either promptly admitting the person or promptly declining to do so. This requires adequate staffing of such admission centers so that the difficult choice of which path to follow is promptly taken and the police officers can get on with their duty—either leaving the arrested person under psychiatric care or taking him or her to the police booking station.

If the mental health path is followed and the patient admitted, this does not preclude the person's immediate or subsequent placement in the community, in his home, if he has one, or elsewhere, subject to whatever conditions are appropriate to a post-hospital placement. Further, these psychiatric emergency rooms must be reasonably accessible to police districts, otherwise the line of least effort for the police will be followed too frequently, which is immediate inclusion within the criminal justice system.

Another encouraging path is being pursued to a similar end. Currently several states have established mental health courts. Their broad pattern is that, instead of the police booking station, the police can take the arrested person to the mental health court for decision as to bail or detention and for assessment of the person's suitability to be retained in the mental health system or diverted to the criminal justice system.

Whether a special twenty-four-hour court or improved psychiatric admitting facilities should make this first decision is a matter of difficulty; but that there should be such a decision early after the criminal's arrest seems clear. One way or another, an early decisional process will diminish the number of seriously ill people who sink through the criminal justice system to the maximum security prisons and then on to a grimly punitive supermax.

A concluding note on this topic may be appropriate concerning the dangerousness of the mentally ill. Both as regards violent and nonviolent serious crime, the mentally ill have no higher incidence of such behavior than a random sample of the general population of the same age and socioeconomic circumstances. But mentally ill people who are also abusing alcohol or other drugs do have a higher incidence of violent and serious crime.

We must develop better methods of providing appropriate treatment and appropriate controls of criminals who are seriously mentally ill. The inexorable punitive approach we follow at present is cruel, expensive, and of no social utility.

Deterrence, Rehabilitation, and Prison Conditions

Neither those favoring deterrence nor those favoring rehabilitation seem to recognize that we lack knowledge of the efficacy of these plans and, more surprisingly, that such knowledge could be discovered were we diligent in the matter and followed the path of medicine and its pervasive cohort studies and clinical trials. We pretend there are overwhelming ethical objections to following the path of clinical trials in relation to punishing criminals. It is a strange paradox that on this subject we prefer to rely on selective tales of the "old wives" variety than on planned and effective research. Consequently, to quote George Bernard Shaw: "What do we have other than a wild guess that prisons do more good than harm?"

My opinion about both deterrence and rehabilitation (as purposive elements and justifications of prison regimes) is that both are myths. The threat of punishment, no matter how severe, rarely deterred anyone who believed he could get away with it—and what criminal does not? Only those too overcome by rage or psychiatric disorder to care about the consequences. Some will be deterred and adhere to Sydney Smith's predicted determination not to risk return to such misery, but, in others, their desire not to return will be overwhelmed by the harm the prison did to them. Likewise for rehabilitation: It comes from within, and the best we can do is help the prisoner to help himself. Not an easy task. Overwhelming both deterrence and rehabilitation is the fact of imprisonment, whatever the conditions. Prison adversely affects the self-image of the prisoner and his later behavior. The worse the conditions, the worse the later behavior. But if decent conditions are allowed and self-improvement by way of work, education, and vocational training are available, and their use encouraged, some prisoners will gain from it and be helped to lead conforming and productive lives on release, which they otherwise would not. Whether their move to a better and law-abiding life balances the harm of prison to the mass of prisoners, I know not.

I do know that prison conditions are not the reason why every prisoner I have met counts the days to freedom, and that no prisoner I have ever met consciously wishes to return to prison, though many recognize the likelihood of that occurrence. This suggests that the most fruitful means of reducing recidivism lies with aftercare, with helping the released convict to get a job, a place to stay, and encouraging him to stick to it until he gets on his feet and is committed to the path of righteousness.

It is not violence in prison that engenders a hatred of imprisonment and a powerful longing for freedom. Violence is indeed deeply feared by some convicts and is a cruel infliction on others, but the homicide and serious injury rates are lower behind bars than those in the neighborhoods from which most prisoners now come. And the likelihood of being raped in prison or jail is much exaggerated. It is the degradation of imprisonment itself, its impact on self-image, the separateness from family and friends, and the guilt of having caused harm to them and to others that constitute the larger burdens of prison.

Speaking of harm, at present in the United States the harm that the captivity of two million people in prison does to the community is hard to exaggerate. Nobody really knows the number of families, children, friends, and associates who are adversely affected. We do know that they are overwhelmingly poor and come disproportionately from racial minorities, which gravely compounds the harm to them. Their family structure is shattered, their incomes suffer, their political influence dwindles, and they exist deprived in the land of plenty.

A basic concern of prison commentators in the nineteenth century was the principle of "less eligibility," whose current value is its demonstration that good minds can believe absurd things when they address criminal punishments. "Less eligibility" held that prison conditions must always exceed in adversity those existing in society for the law-abiding poor—such was its mantra. Sydney Smith and Thomas Carlyle (Smith's letter to Sir Robert Peel in Volume I, p. 187, of Sean McConville's *A History of English Prison Administration* [London: Routledge, 1981], and Carlyle's pamphlet referred to in the same volume at p. 356) treated it as an inexorable truth, so that obviously prison conditions must always be more rigorous than those in the workhouse. Were this not so, the "vagabond class" (who were the prevailing terror of the nineteenth-century commentators on prison) would by crime rush to the larger comforts of the prison. Thus, the crank and the treadmill survived through the nineteenth century in prisons since they provided hard labor without productivity, whereas those in the workhouse might see some value in the products of their enforced labor.

Less eligibility was a quaint and early misapplication to the definition of an appropriate prison regime of the idea of the reasonable man of the dismal science, with his simplistic cost-benefit analysis. Much of the less eligibility argument in nineteenth-century England was directed at the prison diet, with comparisons being made between the diet in the workhouse and in the prison, and with official efforts being made to ensure that the prison diet remained more meager and less edible than the workhouse diet. (See *English Local Prisons 1860–1900* by Sean McConville [London: Routledge, 1995].) It has long been rejected by commentators, though it finds its contemporary analog in public political expressions that, given what those in prison and jail have done, they deserve no better.

But suppose we turn this misdirected principle of less eligibility on its head, cannot a more attractive argument be made as follows: By virtue of the enforced banishment of prison and jail, and the full assumption of responsibility for prisoners by the state, should not behind bars be always at least as good as or a little better than the conditions of the worst-off segment of law-abiding members of society for whom no such responsibility has been assumed? Should not the diet in the prison be better than in the workhouse, the labor more productive, the health care more adequate, and so on?

Would this cause a rush of the "vagabond class" to the prisons and jails of the United States? Of course not. To take it to the extreme, one has only to throw open the gates of a prison, any prison, and count how many people rush in and how many rush out. Prison itself, not the conditions within prison, is the essence of punishment.

The lesson for us from our forebears, who adhered to a belief in the doctrine of "less eligibility," is that we too often heed the fearmongers and too easily trade our freedoms for the illusion of security and safety. Governments have never been slow to make the barter, for their nature is to control. What we allow our governments to do to the worst of us sooner or later carries over to increasing segments of the rest of us.

Carrying that idea forward, let me offer a useful test of the details of a sensible prison regime: Assume you are the warden of a prison and have a relatively free hand in setting the conditions of the regime. In your prison, your brother, whom you love, is a prisoner. (The authorities, judicial and administrative, do not know of this relationship, since he had years earlier in his turbulent career changed his name and cut off all official ties with you.) You view his conviction and sentence to imprisonment as entirely appropriate. It will help neither him nor you if you reveal the relationship between you or if you single him out in any way. Now consider the details of the regime you will impose on all your prisoners, including your brother; the disciplinary rules, the adjudicative processes for alleged breaches of those rules, the punishments you will approve for all those so adjudicated as guilty. Consider also what opportunities you will afford all your prisoners for education and self-development. It is a helpful and humanizing exercise. It should define the bottom level of conditions a government should provide for all its prisoners.

That idea leads to a more ambitious reason for concern with prison conditions. Evolutionary biologists tell us that Darwin's phrase, "survival of the fittest," has been widely misapplied. It refers not to the survival of the strongest or the swiftest or the most intelligent. It refers to the survival of species that adapt best to a changing environment. As a species, we now confront a rapidly changing social environment in which ethnic and religious schisms are a major threat to our survival. Biological, chemical, and nuclear weaponry have proliferated to the point where those wishing to express those schisms could, intentionally or not, wipe out humankind. Neither prisons nor societies are likely to survive. If we cannot appreciate and respect the essential humanity of prisoners, we are unlikely to appreciate and respect the essential species bond with those of other backgrounds, other skins, other religions, and other cultures. We had better start at home.